The IEA Health and Welfare Unit

Choice in Welfare No. 12

Families Without Fatherhood

Dedicated to

Robert Andrew Hodkinson

The IEA Health and Welfare Unit

Choice in Welfare No. 12

Families Without Fatherhood

Norman Dennis
George Erdos

IEA Health and Welfare Unit
London, 1992

First published in 1992
by
The IEA Health and Welfare Unit
2 Lord North St
London SW1P 3LB

ISBN 0-255 36273-0

Typeset by the IEA Health and Welfare Unit
in New Century Schoolbook 11 on 12 point
Printed in Great Britain by
Goron Pro-Print Co. Ltd
Churchill Industrial Estate, Lancing, West Sussex

Contents

Acknowledgement

The IEA Health and Welfare Unit is very grateful to the Esmée Fairbairn Charitable Trust for its generous support of our research and educational work for the last three years.

Editor's Foreword

The family is the foundation stone of a free society. In it children learn the voluntary restraint, respect for others and sense of personal responsibility without which freedom is impossible. Yet family life has received surprisingly little attention from the intellectual supporters of liberty. The probable reason is that, until very recently, solid family life could be taken for granted. But today family life is breaking down. One-parent families now make up 19 per cent of all families; some 28 per cent of births now take place outside marriage; and each year about 150,000 additional children under 16 become the victims of divorce. On any reckoning these are dramatic developments which have caused many commentators, whether they incline to socialism or to liberty, to re-think their philosophy.

The term 'underclass' has come into use to describe those groups who live outside the norms of social life: their family life tends to be broken, they rely on welfare benefits rather than work, and they resort to crime and drugs. The IEA Health and Welfare Unit has published Charles Murray's *The Emerging British Underclass* in which he gauges the rise of this group on three measures: illegitimacy, crime and failure to work. The term 'underclass' makes sense as a description of life in some American inner cities, but Dennis and Erdos—despite sharing Murray's concerns—do not accept that the problem can be understood as that of a self-contained inner-city underclass. For them, growing illegitimacy and family breakdown, the reduction in the work ethic and rising crime are signs of a general malaise affecting British culture.

What is also important about their thesis is that Dennis writes as a socialist who is concerned about the decline of socialist morality. His standpoint is that of the ethical socialist (a point of view described in *English Ethical Socialism*, co-authored by Dennis and Professor A.H. Halsey) which is in essence the moral view of the respectable working class, based on solid family life, devotion of parents to their children, hard work, honesty and consideration for neighbours. The Labour party was once the party of such decent, straightforward men and women, but today it has been captured by middle-class intellectuals whose values are very different. To Dennis they are the values of absolute *laissez-faire* in personal lifestyle and, as such, are not compatible with socialist scepticism about *laissez-faire* in economics.

In Dennis' view, socialists can be divided into two groups, 'ethical socialists' and 'egoistic socialists'. The ethical socialists hold that individuals are personally responsible in all social circumstances, whereas the egoistic socialists contend that society, or the environment, or 'the system' cause individuals to behave as they do. For the egoistic socialist, individuals may live whatever lifestyle they choose and if things go wrong or there are casualties, the State should pick up the pieces. They are, according to Dennis, socialist only in that they call for the State—which means other people, the taxpayer—to pick up the bill for their folly. Dennis asks what would happen if everyone took that view: who would be left to care for the casualties? And what are the prospects for a 'caring society' if parents are not inclined to care fully for their own children? Individual freedom, he insists, must be exercised in ways which are compatible with the exercise of like freedom by others.

The division among socialists can also be found among capitalists, or more strictly, classical liberals. The 'egoistic capitalists', more commonly called 'libertarians', believe that people should be able to do as they wish. For some libertarians a bad conscience—guilt they might call it—is in all circumstances as objectionable as State coercion. Other libertarians believe that without State interference human existence would settle down to a natural harmony. People, they say, are essentially good and do not need to be controlled.

If Dennis and Halsey are ethical socialists then classical liberals such as Friedrich Hayek and Michael Novak might be called 'ethical capitalists'. For them, the heart of a free society is personal responsibility guided by conscience. Ethical capitalists represent the mainstream of classical-liberal thought and hold that human imperfection is inescapable. Some people are downright bad and need to be controlled, but the agency of control—the State—should not be trusted with too much power, for it too is affected by human imperfection. Their historic remedy was a 'government of laws' rather than rule by the arbitrary commands of officials. And, no less important, they stressed the importance of an energetic, vital, private moral order built on strong families and vigorous voluntary associations established for the service of one another.

Dennis and Erdos' concluding chapter 'The Intellectuals' New Betrayal' takes to task those opinion leaders who have made it their business to make excuses for what most people regard as unequivocally bad behaviour. Activities like crime and rioting, insist the intellectual elite, are caused by poverty or bad housing. To Dennis, whose working life has been dedicated to studying the family-centred culture of the respectable working class, such claims are without foundation. The unemployed men in the North-East of the 1930s, who faced far greater material hardship and far more real and lasting uncertainty about their futures, did not turn to the 1930s equivalent of ram-raiding to pass their time. They kept their culture of family and neighbourly mutual aid in good order. Thus, for Dennis and Erdos, there is no automatic link between poverty and crime or disorder. Perhaps—they venture to hope—the day is dawning when common sense based on the practical wisdom forged by centuries of experience will be allowed to cast a chink of light on discussions about the family and culture among the intelligentsia.

The IEA never expresses a corporate view but this book, written with the rigour and occasional dry humour characteristic of Norman Dennis, can be wholeheartedly recommended as a scholarly and thought-proving contribution to public debate.

Finally, the fact that Professor A.H. Halsey, a lifelong leader of socialist thought, has been prepared to produce a Foreword testifies to the importance of the issues raised. The decline of the family goes to the heart of Western civilization, presenting challenges for us all, classical liberal and socialist alike.

David G. Green

Foreword

Modern society has strange superstitions. I think the central one is the belief that if ego maximises his or her choices we are all better off. Put more portentously it is the fallacy that individual freedom is a collective good. The family is the age-old disproof of this contemporary nonsense. The traditional family is the tested arrangement for safeguarding the welfare of children. Only a post-Christian country could believe otherwise. The individualist doctrine is an hallucination with two main sources. First is the spectacular advance of human power over nature, which has relieved so many of us from the life of toil that our grandparents had to take for granted. They invented the workplace, the career, the substitutes for human muscle and sweat and we with our micro-chips and washing machines have both inherited and refined these escapes from the 'curse of Adam'. We call it the economy or the productive system and we employ economic statisticians and Treasury politicians to celebrate its continual growth. We use a language of productivity, employment, capital and education which encourages us to imagine that the family has nothing to do with national prosperity.

Then second there is the developing assumption, so rampant in the 1980s, that the adult ego is self-sufficient. Children thereby become commodities—quality objects to be sure—but nonetheless things just like cars or videos or holidays which adults can choose to have in preference to other consumables. And if they do, that is their choice and their responsibility. Contraceptive control of our bodies enhances the illusion. So who needs a family or a community or, for that matter, a government other than to prevent the ruin of the market for these good things by thieves and frauds? Surely technology has conquered nature and we can safely allow individuals to choose a consuming style, limited only by their willingness to work for money. Everybody is then free to buy the good lie of their own definition. Marriage becomes a mere contract.

Our ancestors were poorer but wiser. They understood the notion of political economy. They knew what the modern fantasy forgets, that we are all dependent on one another. Atomized individuals calculate only for themselves and only for their own lives. Yet their very existence depends on calculation across generations. Few women and fewer men would rationally choose to have children in a world of exclusively short-term egoistical calculation. The costs and foregone satisfactions are too high. Hence rich countries which carry the modern ethos have declining or incipiently declining populations. (For a stable population there must be total period fertility rate of 2.1 children per woman; Britain has 1.8, West Germany 1.6, Italy and Spain 1.4 or even 1.2.) The individualized as distinct from socialized country eventually and literally destroys itself.

Nor is this the whole of the modern mirage. In reality the family is part of, not separate from, the economy. Family parents are the main producers of tomorrow's wealth and we all consume what they produce. That is why we need a just political economy to ensure that the beneficiaries pay their dues. Behind the fiscal and monetary facade, old age pensions are dependent on the future work of today's children. Yet paradoxically our political economy, far from paying family parents, actually punishes them for their folly in producing within the framework of the family the producers of the future. Such people as Frank Field on the left, Sir Brandan Rhys Williams on the right and Professor Richard Whitfield in the academic non-political centre have shown that our system of taxation and social security is systematically biassed against the family, and increasingly so since the 1960s.

How can all this be turned round? The first step is to get the facts right. I appreciate that 'facts' always appear in the context of assumptions about what is good or bad for human beings. We deal today with heated value discord in these matters. I share with my colleague Norman Dennis the value position of the ethical socialist as set out in our *English Ethical Socialism* (Oxford University Press, 1988). Central to that position is the doctrine of personal responsibility under virtually all social circumstances. People act under favourable and unfavourable conditions but remain responsible moral agents. History heavily conditions them, their own actions eventually become history and therefore determine the future balance of favour and disfavour in the ceaseless effort to become good people in a good society. The whole question of the quality of life remains for ever open. There are no ineluctable laws of history, only a continual reloading of the dice by millions of individual decisions. It follows that reproductive and family decisions are crucial to human destiny. Whatever the character of society or state, polity or economy, religion or culture, parents cannot escape responsibility for the quality of their children as citizens.

In the light of this political morality I see incontrovertible evidence of a weakening of the norms of the traditional family since the 1960s. It is not that I see a golden age of traditionalism. Material deprivation, and inequality between the classes and the sexes were integral to British society in the first half of the century. There was no utopia. There was cruelty, a double standard of sexual morality, incest and child abuse, savage treatment of unmarried mothers, desertions and separations. Nevertheless the traditional family system was a coherent strategy for the ordering of relations in such a way as to equip children for their own eventual adult responsibilities.

The much-needed reform of the system required comprehensive strengthening of supporting health, education and security services if quality children were to be produced, women were to have freedom to combine motherhood with career and men were to be encouraged to take a fuller part in the domestic rearing of their offspring. Instead the evidence of more recent change is that the supporting services have deteriorated, the increment of economic growth has been transferred disproportionately to the individual pocket horizontally and to the rich vertically through the running down of family allowances, the raising of regressive national insurance contributions, the abandoning of joint taxation for spouses, the failure to fund adequate community care, and so on. In the 1980s the economic individual has been exalted and the social community desecrated. Paradoxically, Mrs Thatcher may well be seen by dispassionate future commentators as a major architect of the demolition of the traditional family. For, by an irony of history, while Mrs Thatcher forbore to extend the ethic of individualism into domestic life, and tacitly accepted that the family was the one institution that properly continued to embrace the sacred as distinct from the contractual conception of kinship, those who denounced her doctrines of market-controlled egoism with the greatest vehemence were also those who most rigorously insisted on modernizing marriage and parenthood along her individualistic and contractual lines. The opposite might have been expected. A thorough anti-Thatcherism, far from introducing egoistic calculation into the family, would logically have lauded the other-regarding spouse, parent, child or sibling and advocated the extension of the principle of altruism into the other institutions of a socialist commonwealth. Thus it was that Mrs Thatcher inadvertently found her central principles powerfully supported in this crucial area by quite other social and personal forces in the creation of a new and indeed unprecedented wave of pro-individual, anti-social development of economy, polity and community.

No one can deny that divorce, separation, birth outside marriage and one-parent families as well as cohabitation and extra-marital sexual intercourse have increased rapidly. Many applaud these freedoms. But what should be universally acknowledged is that the children of parents who do not follow the traditional norm (i.e. taking on personal, active and long-term responsibility for the social upbringing of the children they generate) are thereby disadvantaged in many major aspects of their chances of living a successful life. On the evidence available such children tend to die earlier, to have more illness, to do less well at school, to exist at a lower level of nutrition, comfort and conviviality, to suffer more unemployment, to be more prone to deviance and crime, and finally to repeat the cycle of unstable parenting from which they themselves have suffered.

Dennis and Erdos do not propose to review all the evidence. There is, for example, also recent work by Kathleen Kiernan on the impact of family disruption in childhood on transitions made in young adult life (*Population Studies*, 46, 1992). And there is the sophisticated analysis by James Coleman and his associates in Chicago (*Resources and Actions: Parents, their Children and Schools*, a report to the National Science Foundation and National Center for Educational Statistics, August 1991) which describes the relation between family structure and educational performance in the United States. The evidence all points in the same direction, is formidable, and tallies with common sense.

The focus has generally been upon the benefits of the decline of the family for formerly oppressed women and for young men and women freed from the social control of extra-marital sexual activity. Alternatively it has been upon the losses suffered by children. Dennis and Erdos draw particular attention to an overlooked consequence of family breakdown—the emergence of a new type of young male, namely one who is both weakly socialized and weakly socially controlled so far as the responsibilities of spousehood and fatherhood are concerned. That is just another way of saying that he no longer feels the pressure his father and grandfather and previous generations of males felt to be a responsible adult in a functioning community. But we must be clear what the thesis does not say. The comparison is of averages. It is not maintained that traditionally reared children will all be healthy, intelligent and good; nor that children from parentally deprived homes will all turn out to be sickly, stupid and criminal; nor that all male youths who do not intend to marry have an appetite for destruction. Like all social science the relevant studies deal with multiple causes of multiple effects and give us estimates of statistical association for particular groups at particular moments in history. Nevertheless it must be insisted that no contrary evidence is available to contradict the average differences postulated by the stated thesis. Accordingly the conclusion must be drawn that committed and stable parenting must be a priority of social policy. If that view is accepted, it is no comfort either to the right or the left. Committed parenting cannot be the outcome of the market policies of economic liberals nor of what Norman Dennis has dubbed the 'egoistic socialism' of irresponsible fathers. The challenge to social policy is to avoid both of these evils.

A.H. Halsey

The Authors

Norman Dennis was born in 1929 and spent his childhood in various working-class neighbourhoods during the depression years in Sunderland, County Durham, a sea-faring, ship-building and coal-mining town on the north-east coast of England. A crucially formative year was spent at the beginning of the Second World War living with a coal-miner's family in a small colliery village, Leasingthorne, County Durham. Admitted from Sunderland's grammar school to Corpus Christi College, Oxford, he preferred to study at the London School of Economics of Tawney, Popper, Ginsberg and Laski. He has been a Ford Fellow, Rockefeller Fellow, and Fellow of the Center for Advanced Study in the Behavioural Sciences at Palo Alto, California. He has carried out research into working-class communities from the Universities of Leeds, Bristol, Birmingham, Durham and Newcastle. Married with two children and one grandchild, he is currently Reader in Social Studies at the University of Newcastle upon Tyne.

George Erdos was born in 1946 in Hungary and he spent his formative years there. He left in 1964. Having finished secondary school in Germany, he studied at the universities of Frankfurt, New Hampshire, Bar-Ilan, Mainz and Cambridge. He settled in England and teaches psychology at the University of Newcastle upon Tyne. He is married with three children.

Having experienced the repercussions of Communism and —albeit indirectly—Fascism, he saw at first hand that dictatorship is too high a price to pay for individual security. But in order for democracy to work, weak external controls have to be coupled with strong internal controls—thus his interest in socialization. He is a firm adherent of the tenets of ethical socialism.

From 1985 onwards he taught in three intensive summer courses of the Educational Opportunity Programme at Rutgers University in Newark, New Jersey. Its basis was that, by supporting him in obtaining a degree, the Afro-American male would be assimilated to the norms of the white middle class, and be enabled to enjoy success in American terms. This experience brought Dr Erdos into close contact with the victims of urban poverty and sensitized him to the complex problem of cause and effect in the cycle of deprivation. The problem that remained with him from that experience, and gave him his interest in the role of the male in modern society, was the fact that the programme was targeted at Afro-American men, but was utilized with enthusiasm not by the male, but by the Afro-American female participants.

Preface

On 9 September 1991 rioting broke out at Meadow Well in North Tyneside, just to the east of the shipbuilding district of Wallsend and the old mining settlement of Percy Main, and just to the west of the deep-sea fishing and shiprepairing port of North Shields.

One of the authors is a native of a similar general area about six miles to the south, the City of Sunderland. He had lived on a notoriously bad housing estate in Bristol, Southmead, for more than a year in the 1950s. It was one of the two worst housing estates in the city. As part of his research, he had participated in local life, as well as interviewing people in their houses, often for hours at a time. He was the sociologist with the Bristol Social Project, which was designed to apply the techniques of improvement elaborated by the Chicago Social Area Projects of the previous twenty years or so.

Two days after the riot took place, he cycled to South Shields, took the 'Sheila Cunningham' over the Tyne, and turned off the Howden Road into the estate of twelve-to-an-acre, mainly semi-detached dwellings, all with gardens. (In the 1930s it was taken for granted that it was highly desirable to provide working people with the means not only of occupying their leisure time, especially in periods of unemployment, but also with the means of sustenance.)[1]

The first thing he saw, at the entrance to the estate, was a burnt-out Pakistani-owned shop. The streets were strewn with broken glass and other rubbish. About 20 per cent of the houses were boarded-up, perhaps a higher proportion. Some of the houses were burned-out. Some roofs had collapsed. The author was looking for a particular house, the home of one of the young men whose death in a car-chase was the cause of the riot. The *Shields Gazette* had a report that it now displayed a protest notice, saying 'Police Murderers'. After a while he asked a passer-by where the house was.

'He didn't live here. His house is the other side of Smith's Park station, over there. *Where the riots were.*'

'Where the riots were! Isn't this where the riots were, then?'

'This is South Meadow Well. The riots were on North Meadow Well.'

'Well, what about the burnt-out houses? All the glass on the road here? That shop?'

'That's normal. That's happening all the time.'

All this would have been completely incredible at the time of the author's research in the 1950s.

Himself born in the closely-knit shipbuilding community of Millfield, Sunderland, and married to a Sunderland coal-miner's daughter, he had been in a sense for forty years the sociologist of the respectable working class. His first piece of research was a participant-observation study of a coal-mining town in Yorkshire, published as *Coal is Our Life*. He went on to Bristol to live not only in Southmead, but for several months in Lockleaze, studying there a thriving council-estate community. He then examined the clash between the Sunderland planners and Millfielders over so-called 'slum' clearance in the 1960s and 1970s. In the late 1980s he was co-author with A.H. Halsey of a book examining the political philosophy of the respectable working-class's outlook, 'chapel and temperance socialism'.[2] His collaboration with A.H. Halsey on these topics, and this central concern, has been continuous, formally or informally, for thirty of those years.

The other author of the present work is a social psychologist. He was born in Hungary, and his childhood and early youth familiarized him with an entirely different state of affairs, communist totalitarianism. Through his German relatives and their fate he also had known only too well the history of Nazism, and not abstractly.

The remoter origin of this volume lies in our long-standing joint interest in the conditions of decent community life. Fatherlessness came up as an aspect of this when an IEA/Joseph Rowntree Foundation seminar was held in November 1990, the intention of the organizers being to explore any grounds for consensus between the political left and right on the subject of the modern family. One of the authors was invited to prepare a paper for the seminar based upon a very extensive study of the literature on the lone-parent family. Contrary to the near-consensus among his social policy colleagues that, in its strongest version, it was reactionary nonsense to allege that the lone-parent family was inferior to the two-parent family, he could find no study which did not show clearly that, over a whole range of outcomes, children in lone-parent families suffered disabilities as compared with the average child in the stable two-parent family.

In a weaker version of the consensus it was assumed that, in so far as there were differences, these were not due to lone-parenthood as such, but merely to low income. Alternatively or additionally, they were due to the fact that the non-academic public erroneously believed that lone-parenthood was to the disadvantage of children, and this erroneous belief itself, this stigma, had the effect of creating disadvantage. There was nothing a dollar and a dose of enlightenment would not fix.

Colleagues holding this view were asked for bibliographical details of the studies that supported either the stronger version or the weaker version—at that stage fully expecting that such studies were available. On one occasion this bona fide request was met, surprisingly, with a hostile, 'You know quite well that there are no such studies!' Several, however, were able to point to research which did show that *some* lone-parent families or other form of alternative family did a better job than *some* stable heterosexual two-parent families, that *some* children benefited from the divorce of their quarrelling parents, and so forth.

But this was simply an example of *ignoratio elenchi*—answering a question that has not been asked. No one with any knowledge of social statistics would have expected any different result. Measures of the frequency of any characteristic in different social groups nearly always greatly overlap: that is a function of the complexity of social causation. In comparing two populations, therefore, it is normally easy to show 'good' results at the *best* end of the *worst* distribution, and 'bad' results at the worst end of the best distribution.

In considering the past twenty or thirty years—to give an arbitrary start to the period, let us say from the availability of the Djerassi oral contraceptive pill in 1960—who has benefited and who has lost by the changes in family life? Women on the whole have gained much of the ground they have fought over. In that sense at least we can say they are beneficiaries of the sexual revolution and the loosening of the bonds of kinship.

The results for children are the subject of much discussion. We do not attempt to present all the evidence, which in our opinion points repetitively in the same direction. We merely take two typical large-scale studies. One of them was chosen because it showed the state of social science knowledge, as well as that of common experience, at the time when the institutions of family life were so cheerfully being dismantled by academia and the media. (Chapter 4.) The other was chosen to a small degree because it dealt with family life in our home-base, Newcastle upon Tyne, but mainly because it brought up to the present day the experience of fatherlessness in the lives of people now in their thirties. (Chapter 5.)

Those who dismiss these studies as being 'out of date' have a puzzling notion of the value of their own evidence for saying that. For to know that they are right about the lack of harm to today's generation of children brought up in families lacking fatherhood, they themselves will have to wait for another thirty years in order to see how things have worked themselves out empirically all the way into adulthood. In other words, we have strong evidence of what has happened up to now. They have only assertions about what they believe will happen in the future if their nostrums are adopted.

These matters are fought out under the conventional banners of the 'left' and 'right' in politics. But Chapter 6 shows that, where the family is concerned, there is a strange reversal of roles. The 'right' has taken a collectivist stand and the 'left' has taken what is in substance a 'free market' stand—a point made powerfully by Lord Young of Dartington (Michael Young), the Director of the Institute of Community Studies and founding Chairman of the Social Science Research Council.[3]

Changes in the family have not only affected husbands, wives, fathers, sons, daughters, brothers, sisters, and the web of kinship roles created by conventional Christian marriage. They have also affected neighbours and fellow-citizens. In Chapter 7 we deal with the spectacular increases in crime and generally the resistible rise of the obnoxious English man in the last generation. We speculate that to find the cause of a rapidly increasing phenomenon it is futile and foolish to seek it in factors which may be, or are, in themselves social problems, such a 'poverty', 'unemployment', 'bad housing' and so forth, but which have not been increasing, either phenomenologically or in reality, on anything like the same scale. The notable aspect of national life that has been dramatically changing at the same time as civil life has been deteriorating is the family. The change to which we direct particular attention is the progressive liberation of young men (partly at the insistence of women themselves) from the expectation that adulthood involves life-long responsibility for the well-being of their wife, and fifteen or twenty years of responsibility for the well-being of their children. The hypothesis that young men who are invited to remain in a state of permanent puerility will predictably behave in an anti-social fashion is outlined in Chapter 8.

We suggest that the changes in perception that have strengthened the forces of egoism, and indeed of nihilism, did not originate with the poor, the unemployed and the ill-housed. No one detests the minority of those who are for the time being acting as nihilistic thieves and louts more heartily than the poor, unemployed and ill-housed majority who have the misfortune to be living near them. They are not an underclass either in the sense that they form the majority of people in any area, or in the sense that they have *themselves* created a culture distinct from and in opposition to a dominant culture.[4] Those who are for the time being behaving in a nihilistic, thieving or loutish mode have at their disposal only very limited technical and personal resources for changing public attitudes in favour of their lifestyles. But there is a category of anti-social actions, carried out by a changing and fluid set of carriers of those actions (whether or not the carriers of those actions are designated an underclass is then merely a matter of terminology, not of substance) and the number of these anti-social actions has been increasing rapidly. Attention must inevitably fall, therefore, on the role of the intelligentsia, in so far as it has spoken out or remained silent, in bringing about the substantial changes in family culture and structure and their train of consequences. (Chapter 9.)

Underlying all these issues are broader questions of the taken-for-granted philosophy that reigns in a society, and these are dealt with in Chapters 1, 2 and 3.

The Meadow Well riots then crystallized our common concern with this basic sociological and social-psychological problem. To what extent is the widespread and deep acceptance of certain values of civility necessary for the existence of a prosperous society of free and tolerant people, keeping it from the horrors of totalitarian uniformity on the one side, and the consequences of unbridled selfishness on the other?

Our first consideration brought us to the question of the extent to which the idea of 'social values' had itself been eroded during the time between the study of the 'bad' estate of Southmead, which by the standards of the early 1990s would have looked almost entirely civilized, and its equivalent only a generation later, Meadow Well. It is to this question that we now turn.

Norman Dennis
George Erdos

Notes

1 By 1990 the net income of a married man on average hourly male earnings for all industries and services, with a non-earning wife and two children under 11 meant that it took him 3 minutes to earn a pint of fresh milk. It took him 5 minutes to earn a large loaf of white sliced bread, 11 minutes to earn a pint of draught beer, 12 minutes to earn a dozen eggs, and 13 minutes to earn 500 grams of butter. (The equivalent figures twenty years before had been milk 5 minutes, bread 9 minutes; beer 14 minutes; eggs 22 minutes; butter 19 minutes.) (*Social Trends 1992, No. 22*, London: HMSO, 1991.) By contrast, in 1991 it took a University lecturer in the Sudan 1.5 hours to earn a pint of milk—and a general labourer a full day. It took the lecturer 2.5 hours' work to earn a dozen eggs, and three days' work to earn a jar of Nescafe. ('Cost of Living Index', *Sudan Monitor*, March 1991, p. 2.)

In England, gardens attached to dwellings for the purposes of providing sustenance for a poor family had therefore become a historical curiosity.

As for the garden's function as a leisure pursuit, at the time of the visit to the riot estate an institution no less 'respectable' than the Prudential insurance company, using a medium no less powerful than a television advertisement, was mocking the idea:

Young man (in stupid voice): We want to enjoy the *garden!*
Young woman (sharing her mockery with the audience, but not with her 'boy friend'): I want to be able to *stuff* the garden, and go on a world cruise.
The Prudential announces approvingly that more and more young women are taking their (non-gardening) fate into their own hands.

   None of the gardens seen by the author on his visit were cultivated for any purpose, whether aesthetic or utilitarian, though no doubt closer inspection with this in mind would have revealed some.

2 *Coal Is Our Life*, London: Eyre and Spottiswoode, 1956, with Slaughter, C., and Henriques, F.; *People and Planning*, London: Faber and Faber, 1970; *Public Participation and Planners' Blight*, London: Faber and Faber, 1972; *English Ethical Socialism*, Oxford: Oxford University Press, 1988, with Halsey, A.H.

3 Lord Young of Dartington, *A Haven in a Heartless World: the Future of the Family*, London: ESRC, 6 December 1990.

4 It is curious to read some accounts of horrific brutality inflicted on, say, the helpless old, on, say, some council estate, brutality and predation of a kind and frequency virtually unknown a generation ago. By being put in the context of the underclass thesis to which the writer concerned is hostile, the question of whether such events are much more numerous today than in the past is confused with the question of whether an 'underclass', as defined by the writer, exists or not. On proving that horrific attacks are still a rarity even in the most dangerous neighbourhoods, and most people there are never brutal and are usually honest, the thesis of the underclass is dismissed—and with it the significance of the decrease of security of person and property. See, for example, Bob Holman, 'Poverty is First among Crimes', *Guardian*, 24 June 1992. Dr. Holman was formerly Professor of Social Work at the University of Bath, and at the time of writing 'Poverty is First among Crimes' was a neighbourhood worker in Easterhouse, Glasgow.

1

Thou Shalt Not Commit
A Value Judgement

In their everyday contacts people make a distinction between how people in need should be treated. On the one hand there is someone who is in need of help now because he has lost out in taking the predictable risks of his own conduct. At the extreme of this category is the person who has ruthlessly pursued his own immediate pleasures and flaunted what other people have advised him is bad practice. He suffers what those to whom he now looks for assistance have all along assumed, and impressed upon him, would be the almost certain disastrous consequences of that conduct. On the other hand is someone upon whom catastrophe has fallen completely out of the blue. At the extreme of this category is the person who now requires assistance, even though he has done everything that wise foresight demanded, diligent skill could achieve, and his society has required of him. (The type-case is Job.)

Presented with two such equally suffering but otherwise contrasted claimants upon his income, wealth, time and compassion, a certain kind of philosopher repudiates common sense. He argues that the personalities and actions of both of them are the product of the infinitely complex interaction that has taken place between the genes each has inherited and the countless, mainly ungraspable, series of external circumstances, including his mother's womb,[1] which have acted upon those genes. The product of each moment of interaction, the 'readiness to act in a certain way'—the personality—at that moment, interacts anew with new circumstances. 'Every instant is the cradle of the next.'[2] The personality responds and interacts always and inevitably in the one and only way in which the given personality could possibly perceive, evaluate and interact with the entirely given, entirely external circumstances of that same moment. The personality that develops out of that interaction then interacts once more with the new environment. Within certain limits this environment is sought out or not shunned by that personality making the only choices it possibly could, given the stimulus. This unbroken and unbreakable chain of cause and effect endures for him as long as his life lasts; and all the effects of his having lived will reverberate *ad infinitum*. There is no room for free will, *and therefore no basis for praise or blame*.[3]

In the details of his everyday life, as he lives it with other people face-to-face, even this philosopher is not indifferent to any of even the slightest nuances of desert. He reacts with approval or disapproval, with a readiness to grant or withhold condemnation, to the finest details of tone of voice and body language.

But the more remote, indirect and difficult to trace are the consequences *to himself* of his not discriminating between the one category of needy person and the other, the easier it is for him to apply his principle that he should not make value judgements.

For the person who is not a philosopher, and therefore not particularly sensitive to logical or other contradictions, it is even easier to be non-judgemental about people afar off, whose conduct does not affect him. But he, like the philosopher, remains very sensitive to other people's slights and selfishness near at hand, and is quite ready to be outraged when he personally is deceived or betrayed.

Yet let us grant the whole of this philosopher's case. Let us assume that he has decisively demonstrated the 'cosmic injustice' of praise and blame, glory and stigma, punishment and reward.[4] It does not at all follow that therefore on moral grounds neither of the two hypothetical persons-in-need must be condemned, and that both must be equally helped.

For by this philosopher's argument everyone is put outside the realm of morality. If the philosopher does help, or does not help, or deliberately exacerbates the suffering of one or the other or both, he also is above praise or blame. He has no basis himself, on his own arguments, for behaving 'morally'. His acts of omission or commission, like theirs, are entirely the unforeseeable but inevitable result of the interplay of his genes, his circumstances, and his constantly developing personality. If on this philosopher's grounds the ordinary criminal is not to blame for his actions, neither is the policeman for fitting up an innocent man or assaulting a prisoner.

Someone observing the on-going system from outside, with full and perfect knowledge of all the interlocking events but with no definitive prior knowledge of what any particular result will be (a hypothetical all-knowing observer), would see that it had, as it happens, by now created participants conscious of the system's operations. These participants had become increasingly able to see how it actually worked, though they were very far from having the hypothetical all-seeing, all-knowing observer's complete knowledge of its operation. They had also become, as a matter of fact, gradually and 'importantly' (though still only feebly) capable of predicting the course of certain events with various degrees of certainty.

The hypothetical all-knowing observer would see that very frequently, also simply as a matter of fact, they subjectively experienced their ignorance of the full flow of cause and effect as 'freedom of choice'. They subjectively experienced their evolved capacity to act on their environment as their 'control' over it. They subjectively felt, frequently, that in their own life they were constantly engaged in 'moral' struggle.

This hypothetical all-knowing observer would see, crucially, that the system actually did include *as causes and effects* systems of 'morality', each with its own detailed pattern of approved and prohibited conduct, its own rewards and punishments, its own objects of stigma and applause, its own degree of strictness and laxity. (Aristotle argues, indeed, that as cause and effect, the belief in free will is essential to the pursuit of the scientific enquiry of deterministic systems.) Equally, he would see whether and to what extent the system had evolved people whose beliefs and actions tended to disrupt and weaken one or all of these patterns of morality. The hypothetical all-knowing observer would see both 'moralizers' and 'anti-moralizers' as each in their own way the nodes of the immense web of causes and effects, from which new effects would radiate. Seeing the whole picture up to and including the present, but not knowing the precise future results beforehand, the hypothetical all-knowing observer would perhaps be interested to observe how things did work themselves out. Would the philosophy of the cosmic injustice of punishment and reward gain ground? The necessary result would be ... what it would be. But there would be a necessary result.[5] Or would the assumptions of 'blameworthiness' and 'praiseworthiness' gain ground? Inevitable (perhaps totally unexpected) concrete results would flow from that eventuality.

Adopting the standpoint of the hypothetical all-knowing observer, the 'moralizing' human actor within the system could only say, 'As a result of factors completely beyond my control, I find myself advocating [let us say for the sake of an example] an Apollonian morality of self-restraint and sobriety within a rule-bound and rule-respecting life. Against me are the Dionysian lords of misrule who, also as a result of factors completely beyond their control, are advocating or by their example engendering a life of self-indulgence and anarchy. I believe that, if out of all the interplay of history, my doctrine does increase in appeal, then the results will be that fewer people do feel pain, hunger, grief than if the appeal of the Dionysians increases. It will be interesting to see what will result from the endless interplay of cause and effect, of which I with my views and activities am a part.'

The philosophy of cosmic blamelessness, therefore, does not after all lift its adherents above moralizing, if by that is meant engaging in verbal and practical activities on the basis of beliefs and judgements about their empirically good and bad effects on human beings.

Crucially, it does not demonstrate in the slightest degree that the fact of moralizing or not, and the content of the morality propagated, are unimportant in their effects.

For all practical purposes this sophisticated philosophy of the 'blamelessness of the wrong-doer' is irrelevant. On the arguments of that philosophy itself, the 'blamelessness of the wrong-doer' is itself a doctrine evolved in the course of human interaction, destined to have whatever effects it will have.

Another point of view often runs in harness with that of cosmic blamelessness, and operates when the more general argument begins to flag. It is that the network of human and social cause and effect is unimaginably immense and complicated. No one can have any confidence, therefore, that 'good works' will not end by harming the people they are meant to help (or—less frequently heard—that conventionally 'evil works' will not end up by being beneficial to all). It is therefore nobody's business to judge what is right or wrong in another's conduct.

In fact, that is the point of view that most people take most of the time. It is the point of view of the apathetic voter. It is the point of view of the private man who does not intervene, but passes by on the other side when someone else is being robbed or raped.

But it is also the great argument for being neither a nosey-parker, nor a busy-body, nor an intrusive, patronizing 'do-gooder'. It is, above all, the great argument for being tolerant and open to correction. As a corollary, it is the great argument against the use of force, and especially against the use of the power of the State to impose a particular set of values on the State's subjects.

Striking the right balance between intervention and inactivity, between easy mercy and painful strictness, between forgiveness and revenge, between the occasions for war and those for submission have never been easy. If it had been, humankind would have lacked most of its poetry, drama, song, philosophy, religion, politics, morality and variety of cultures.

The one set of thinkers and practitioners to whom this argument, the argument of the pragmatic complexity of situations of cause and effect, is not available, is that composed of those who use it as the basis for indiscriminate 'help'. For by their own assumptions they do not know what may be helpful and what harmful. In particular, it is not available to those who combine a hostility to State control of 'bad' behaviour (because, they argue, there is no way of knowing what bad behaviour is) with approbation of the State's resources being utilized to 'help' all in need, irrespective of the pattern of the difficult-to-calculate long-term effects. If there is no way of saying what is bad, then there is no way of saying what is good.

But these people, too, with their views and activities, will have their results within the pattern of cause and effect. These results (whatever they may turn out to be) will be experienced by people in the present generation and in generations to come as painful or pleasant, as beneficial or disastrous.

There are thus merely two sides engaged in moral struggle. One side bases its judgements on 'non-judgementalism' and its morality on 'not moralizing'. It is unjust either to reward or punish the individual, for he cannot possibly be 'blamed' for what he is and what his life-experiences have made him. Or, because it is impossible to say what will turn out to be right or wrong, one must either remain aloof from all judgements and predictions, or (illogically, for who can say that is 'best'?) treat everyone with the same generosity or harshness. The other side remains within the mind-set of common sense. It explicitly judges and explicitly moralizes.

Whatever may be the correct ultimate philosophical position, moral condemnation and moral approval of different content have their different results, just as failures and refusals to condemn and approve have their characteristic consequences. For all practical purposes, therefore, the two systems are on all fours: both are moralizing systems with concrete effects.

The conclusion of the struggle between them cannot be predicted with any degree of certainty. All that can be asserted with confidence is that the victories of the one or the other are not a matter of causal indifference. To the extent that one advances, the results will be detrimental to human life, in the sense of the increase in suffering and a decrease in happiness in the world. To the extent that it is defeated, the effects in the lives of human beings will be beneficial. Only those who experience the eventual results will be able to say which side was right and which wrong.

Notes

1 In large American cities such as New York, Washington, Los Angeles and Detroit, by the early 1990s a number of children were being born who were affected by the illicit drugs taken by their mothers during pregnancy. (An assumption about what is now known as the foetal alcohol syndrome—the effects of that legal drug—had been part of the folk-wisdom of ancient Greece in at the latest by Aristotle's time. It was of course very much part of the folk-wisdom of the respectable working class in this country earlier in the twentieth century, and helps explain the 'sexist' disapproval of women drinking in public houses and working men's clubs.) '375,000 American babies were infected in the womb by one or more illicit drugs in 1991. The most frequent was cocaine. In big cities ... the figure is as high as 20 per cent of all babies born.' By 1991, also, the physically deformed and behaviourally difficult drug-exposed children specifically of mothers who had smoked the cocaine derivative 'crack' were reaching the American schools. (*Sunday Times*, 8 March 1992.) Presumably the spread of the seriousness of the degree to which the babies were affected is from the very slight to the severely handicapped. Whatever the accuracy of the figures of the seriousness of this particular problem, such children illustrate the point about the cosmic blamelessness of the what are journalistically labelled 'crack kids', the 'biological underclass', 'the children of the damned' etc.

2 Der Augenblick ist die Wiege einer Zukunft. The phrase in Grillparzer's. *(Das goldene Vlies,* Part III, Act I, lines 114-15.)

3 Such a philosopher's point of view does not imply that all events can be known or calculated. There is no assumption that all physical and human action can be understood in terms of a complex web of cause and effect—only that both physical and human action are a complex web of cause and effect. It has nothing to do with any claim that by the acceptance of universal determinism human affairs are rendered more predictable. Human affairs are no more, and they are no less, predictable for a philosopher adopting this stance than they are for any one else using the techniques which enable more or less sound judgements to be made on the basis of observation, experiment, statistics and experience of how in certain circumstances a personality or group of such-and-such a composition will behave under such-and-such conditions. If he is sober a man will know he is somewhat more likely to be knocked over by a bus than if he is drunk. But drunk or sober, the criss-crossing events are innumerable and mostly untraceable that eventually bring a massive force carried on pneumatic tyres, propelled by an internal combustion engine, driven by a more or less alert man or woman, who is following a bureaucratically determined route and schedule, into violent contact with his body. The complexity of the events bringing him there, and the bus there, in such a way that there is an 'accident', is such that from the point of view of its predicability it does not

matter whether it is thought of as 'an Act of God', or 'a random event', or a 'totally determined occurrence' in which the 'free will' of no individual had any part to play whatsoever.

4 Something like his case is very commonly taken for granted (though not always well-thought through or even consciously present) in many contemporary discussions. It forms the articulated or inarticulate major premise of various species of moral relativism and nihilism represented in assorted centres of influence, from social policy and education to the dramatic arts.

A competing philosophical system, from the opposite point of view, is equally unfriendly to morality. Twentieth-century physics shows the complete unpredictability, even in principle, of sub-atomic particles (the idea is familiar through the best sellers of Stephen Hawking). On that analogy, each individual at each 'moment of decision' behaves like the unpredictable particle. As the decision does not flow from his personality, but is a random event, he cannot be held responsible for it.

5 That 'everything is determined' need not lead to a regime of less praise and blame is argued in one of the most celebrated of sociological analyses, Weber's *The Protestant Ethic and the Spirit of Capitalism* (1904-05), New York: Charles Scribner, 1958.

2

Residues of Judgementalism

In the twentieth century there has rarely been any difficulty about identifying an undeserving rich, any more than there was in previous centuries. But difficulties have arisen over the question of the undeserving and the deserving poor. In discussions of this matter the proponents of the cosmic meaninglessness of praise and blame, reward and punishment, have been strongly represented (and broadly victorious) ever since their battles against the late-nineteenth-century philosophy and methods of Octavia Hill and the Charity Organization Society.[1] Increasingly, reactions strongly reminiscent of moral indignation and moral revulsion greeted those residual and ever-more-rare definitions of poverty which still saw it as a moral matter, where the establishment of certain facts enabled a distinction to be made, and that the distinction involved also moral judgements.

These residual moral definitions of poverty depended upon a belief that there was a numerous—certainly potentially numerous—category of people whose misfortune stemmed from their own conduct. Their gambling, drinking and work habits, for example, threatened the vulnerable standards and fragile achievements of other groups in similar economic, locality and housing situations. To what extent, and under what conditions should this group be protected from the hardships of their situation by their fellow-citizens? The bereaved, the mentally and physically ill-endowed or damaged, the aged—these were in a different category altogether. Their poverty was a matter of misfortune through no fault of their own.

The notion of voluntary conduct (either vicious or virtuous) was the way in which the necessity for judgementalism was conceptualized by the respectable working class in England in the second half of the nineteenth and the first half of the twentieth century, and by very many other thinkers and cultures at other times and in other places. From the point of view of the hypothetical all-knowing observer the true distinction, however, is not between the consequences of 'voluntary' conduct as against the consequences of external events. All consequences are equally determined and outside the realm of the individual's free choice. *The distinction is between a web of cause and effect in which socially-imposed indoctrination and sanctions play a part, and a web of cause and effect where they do not play a part.*

Thus there is a class of events that has three characteristics. First, people experience them as undesirable and if possible to be avoided. (Some judgements of what is undesirable and if possible to be avoided are very widespread, some quite specific to particular cultures or persons.) Secondly, they are the result of human activity. Thirdly, *that human activity is of the sort that is influenced by the favourable or unfavourable reaction of other people.* The human activity in this case is called a 'vice'.

There is a class of events that shares the last two characteristics (i.e., they are the result of human activity, and are susceptible to control by social training and social control). But they differ on the first. They are experienced as desirable. This human activity is called 'virtuous conduct'.

Where social training and social control are, in the nature of things, ineffective in diminishing the likelihood of the incidence of an event, then common sense attributes the event not to virtue or vice but to the class of events termed 'good fortune' or the class of events termed 'misfortune'.

Of course there are not two clear-cut categories of events, one of events totally insusceptible to social influence, the other of events totally under social control. Each event lies on a continuum, from some point nearer the one extreme, to some point nearer the other. The way in which social indoctrination and social control will have its effects is extremely unpredictable in the case of a single individual, and in many cases uncertain on the social scale. (Prohibition in the United States is the classic example of the latter.) Different value-systems and different technologies alter the position of given events along the continuum. There are probably no empirical examples of either of the pure types. (One can envisage the victim of malaria having escaped his fate if intense social training and severe social control had been directed to prohibitions on any conduct that could possibly bring him into contact with the danger from the disease. One can even imagine social injunctions against growing old leading to marginal extensions in the span of life.)

The distinction between the deserving and the undeserving poor persisted most strongly in that part of the population, the 'respectable' working class, most adversely affected by (to use their 'punitive' and 'judgemental' language) idleness, fecklessness, slovenliness, brutality, squalor, disorder, insobriety, unreliability, debt, incompetence, dirt, destruction and violence. They were affected directly through, for example, the spread of mice and cockroaches, and the bad example set for their children. Indirectly they were affected through the damage to hard-wrought customs and sanctions when too many people flouted or evaded them.

Because of its moral judgementalism the respectable working class was one of the few groups of the poor and deprived to whom the reforming intelligentsia of non-working-class origin did not—and does not—extend its tolerance. One of the ways in which this anomaly was explained away by the reforming intelligentsia was to characterize respectable English working-class values as 'bourgeois'. They were not really working-class values at all but had been foisted upon them—as if working people had never possessed the wit to discover for themselves through their own experience that there was a great deal to be said, especially in their circumstances, for thrift, prudence, foresight, dependability, and self-improvement. To the extent that these virtues also benefited capitalists, turning the working man into his own slave-driver, and his diligent wife into an unpaid adjunct keeping him well 'serviced' for his exploiters, that was unfortunate. But the respectable working man still thought that he was badly advised by his economic betters in the intellectual vanguard when he was exhorted to cut off his proletarian nose to spite bourgeois faces.

The distinction between conduct on the one hand through which the sufferer was the author of his own misfortunes, and conduct on the other which minimized the chance of misfortune, persisted in one area of life longer than elsewhere. This was the area of sexuality and child rearing. The general concept of 'the deserving poor' had long mouldered in the archives of social policy while the same idea still clung to sex and child-care. It was still considered (especially, again, in the respectable working class) that while social condemnation was not very useful (though not entirely useless) in stopping people being, say, struck by lightning, it was much more (though not entirely) effective in discouraging men from having sexual intercourse in circumstances that facilitated their abandoning responsibility for their children and their children's mothers.

The strength of these ideas here, when they had become so weakened elsewhere, was partly due to the fact that the pleasures of sex, potentially, are peculiarly personal and unsocial, even in heterosexual intercourse. Each can merely use the other for self-centred gratification. It is the type-case of the pleasure principle. The sex drives are peculiarly capable of being partly sublimated and in some people wholly foregone (people often die of hunger, thirst, and cold, few of chastity). But out of control the sexual drives and sexual pleasure can be overwhelming.

Thus the savage Bastardy Act of 1610 attributes the problem of fatherless children to 'lewdness'. Lewdness has considerable attractions—to such an the extent that 'temptation' often operates as a synonym for the temptations specifically of sex—so long as any unwanted after-effects can be avoided or discarded.[2] Most lewdness takes place in private between consenting parties. Broadly, it is a waste of time trying to control the man directly at any stage, or either the man or the woman (or any combination of the sexes) at the stage of intercourse. Most of the control, if control there is to be, must therefore fall upon the pregnant woman—according to the logic of the framers of the Act—for it is with the woman's pregnancy that the lewdness of the man and the woman becomes quite obvious. With pregnancy the fact of the private act becomes public knowledge. It was therefore the lewdness of the mother that the Bastardy Act attacked. The whole weight of social control fell on the only one of the two adults whose denials, unlike the man's, could never carry conviction unless complaint of rape had been made shortly after it had taken place, and not by any means always then.

Partly, the Act said, bastardy was a 'great dishonour of Almighty God'—and for many at that time that was no doubt a cardinal point. But the immediate practical objection which made it the subject of a statute was that 'great charge ariseth upon many places within this realm' because of it. If a man succeeded in pleasuring himself in circumstances which enabled him to escape the burdens of fatherhood, why should another man be made, through taxes, to bear them on his behalf? Community provision there must and will be; but no community provision can be viable that encourages activities in which everyone would prefer to indulge, but from which most people abstain because of the known consequences. Social training and social control had failed to deter *her*. Her harsh treatment, including the harsh treatment of her child, would contribute to the deterrence of *others*. That was the spirit of the Bastardy Act.

The same attitudes and logic can be discerned over two centuries later in the evidence of a witness to the Poor Law Commission of 1834. Many women, the witness claimed, could be socially deterred from becoming an unmarried mother. As sensible women do, she could wait to become a mother until after she had succeeded in 'procuring to herself and her child the assistance of a husband and father'. There could be no reason (it became a familiar phrase) for giving to 'vice' the privileges due only to 'misfortune'.[3]

Notoriously these attitudes were still to be found far into the twentieth century. The paper on cohabitation issued by the Supplementary Benefits Commission in 1971 said:

> It would not be right, and we believe that public opinion would not accept, that the unmarried 'wife' should be able to claim benefit denied to a married woman because her husband was in full time work ... Critics of the cohabitation rule ... must demonstrate that society as a whole believes that men and women not married to each other should be given privileges ... for which married couples are not eligible.

Going into the last quarter of the century, a woman social-policy academic in good standing in her profession, Professor

Juliet Cheetham, was still able to write that, in the treatment of the unmarried mother, 'it would be a mistake to imagine that exhortations for economy have always been based on plain meanness'. There was also, she said, the matter of 'fairness' in the distribution of welfare.

But the essential point was that the effects of welfare provision on respect for and adherence to rules whose worth has been demonstrated by general experience had to be considered. Of course there was always a quota of hard cases—a quota of tragedies—but the rule was there to prevent the many more hard cases which would result from the rule disappearing. 'A society's welfare system must not appear to undermine one of its basic units' (not to speak of actually succeeding in undermining it).

There was only the beginning of the tendency, on the grounds they were both 'lone parents', to assimilate the widow to the never-married mother. (The assimilation was virtually total by the early 1990s.) The distinction between them had been considered altogether more important. The widow was the victim of bereavement. No government policy or public stigma could control that phenomenon. But the unmarried mother was paying the price for her own pleasure and folly, and if she was imitated the price of pleasure and folly would rise ever higher. The welfare state therefore provided without public controversy least for the single mother and most for the bereaved family.

It was only at about the time that Cheetham was writing this, 1976, that concern had significantly grown in the previous few years that the welfare of neither the mother nor child should depend upon 'the legal status of the parents' relationship'.[4] The redundancy of the category of deserving and undeserving had at long last reached the family.

Notes

1 Octavia Hill, a disciple and friend of John Ruskin, was one of those who built up the COS on the principle that there was indeed a continuum among the poor: from those poor, in common sense terms, through no fault of their own, to those who, in common sense terms, stubbornly adhered to a way of life that kept them poor. The COS, she argued, should concentrate on the those people who would respond to the methods used and the assistance afforded by the COS in such a way to escape from poverty or, if incapacitated by handicap, illness or old-age, neither waste the help nor use it to make their own conditions worse (e.g. by spending the money on alcohol). The careless and the undeserving must be left to the deterrent regime of the Poor Law. (Bell, E.M., *Octavia Hill: A Biography*, London: Constable, 1942.)

2 By the 1990s it seemed to be almost consensual that to give the control of sexuality a *central* place in the scheme of socialization and social control was a quaint error of our ancestors. Modern experience, of the benefits of controlling it much less, had exposed it and corrected it at last.

To mark the end of his first year in office, Dr George Carey as Archbishop of Canterbury said that the Church was 'just as guilty as any other section of the community in thinking sexual sins more significant than other sins'. The Church ought to be more interested in problems such as global poverty. (*The Independent*, 20 March, 1992.)

The main leader reinforced the point about the near-incomprehensibility of the centrality of sexual controls by turning the argument gently back to the Archbishop. It was the Church which had 'always been obsessed' with the attempt to control sexual desire. The only evidence the leading article adduced was that the Ten Commandments prohibited adultery and the coveting of a neighbour's wife or maid.

Far stronger evidence would have been the Sermon on the Mount, in which Jesus is reported as making the rule altogether stricter, by extending it to even the desire to commit adultery. (Matthew, 5, 17 and 27-8.) But to the extent that the controls of sexuality were necessary for the preservation of very long-term relationships connected with the upbringing of helpless infants and the provision between adults of non-purchaseable face-to-face services, to that extent the Church's guilt is mitigated. Perhaps the Ten Commandments (and their equivalents in other great religions of the world) had appealed across societies and generations because they did represent better intuitive insights into the lessons to be drawn from the experience of both human nature and social organization (including the experience of loyalty required to produce people who care about world poverty) than those of the post-1960s commentators who argued that the centrality accorded such injunctions was obsolete.

3 The witness himself is reported as saying 'the privileges *denied* to misfortune'.

4 Cheetham, J., 'Pregnancy in the Unmarried: The Continuing Dilemmas for Social Policy and Social Work', in Halsey, A.H., *Traditions of Social Policy: Essays in Honour of Violet Butler*, Oxford: Blackwell, 1976, pp. 148-49.

3

Self-Interest, Easy Virtue And Social Costs

People have the task of moulding the members of each new generation so that a sufficiently high proportion of them will be effective actors within the formal institutional arrangements and informal usages of the society in which they live. What a 'sufficiently' high proportion is, can only be known after the event. At the level serving for the time being as the bench mark of success, did the society in fact continually create the capacity to feed, clothe, house, and otherwise provide necessities, conveniences and luxuries for the population, generation by generation? In order to be effective co-operators, the newcomers must be prepared to respond to the changing stream of people with whom they come into contact in ways that are socially defined as appropriate. Whether a social system is changing slowly or rapidly, to meet the needs of its members for an extended period of time it must succeed in establishing in its participants one out of the many but limited viable mixes of self- and other-regarding ideas, feelings, actions, motivations, and skills. 'The characters of men', as Adam Smith said, 'as well as the contrivances of art, or the institutions of civil government, may be fitted either to promote or disturb the happiness both of the individual and of the society.'[1] Some of these defined ways of responding to other people are quite general to all contacts within any given society, and quite general, too, across all societies.

Unless an appropriate pattern of ideas, attitudes and actions is established in the psyche of the participants in the social system, the social system and its participants will sooner or later cease to exist. At the mildest the social system will cease to exist because it has been replaced by that of its conquerors. At the worst the participants themselves will perish through foreign wars, civil strife, pestilence and starvation. 'The inhabitants of the villages ceased, they ceased in Israel.'[2] What in any set of circumstances an 'appropriate' pattern has been can only be definitely assessed when the results are known.

There are some human actions that are intentionally conducted to secure the interests of the individual himself at the expense of the interests of other individuals. A second set of actions are carried out to secure the interests of the individual, but without harming those of others. In the third class, pursuit of the individual's own advantage in important and numerous cases actually furthers the interests of others. A fourth class of actions involves the individual's sacrifice of his own interests in order that he might bring benefit to others. Finally, there are actions that are directed at improving or maintaining the fabric of rules which specify the ways in which people will co-operate with (and oppose) one another.[3]

For brevity those located towards one end of the scale will be called self-regarding, and those towards the other, collectivity-regarding.

At right angles to this scale, so to speak, is another continuum of social action, stretching from social action that places few, to social action that places many demands upon the actor's capacity for far-sightedness and self-restraint.

These distinctions were central to the work on the subject of socialization of one of the most influential of the American sociologists on the far side of the water-shed of the 1960s, Talcott Parsons. His terms were 'ego-oriented' conduct *versus* 'alter-oriented' *versus* 'collectivity-oriented' conduct, and 'expressive' *versus* 'instrumental' conduct.[4] But exactly the same ideas are to be found in plain English in the work of the author already referred to, Adam Smith. Moreover, what Adam Smith has to say about the importance of socialization and social control, and about the indispensability in any successful society of other-regarding and collectivity-regarding conduct seems to be especially persuasive. For he is generally believed to be one of the foremost exponents in the history of social thought—quite erroneously, as we shall show—of the absolute pre-eminence and self-sufficiency of rational egoism. It is therefore Smith's version that will be preferred.

What motivations and skills must be inculcated into each new generation to ensure that the social system will be capable of producing the means of subsistence, health, and safety?

Certain clearly self-regarding motivations, skills and actions are also of crucial social importance. Smith points to certain virtues principally 'useful to oneself' which are at the same time crucial for others and for the maintenance of the structured relationships of a society. First of all there is 'superior wisdom and understanding, by which we are capable of discerning the remote consequences of all our actions, and of foreseeing the advantage or detriment which is likely to result from them'. Secondly, there is 'self-command, by which we are enabled to abstain from present pleasures or to endure present pain, in order to obtain a greater pleasure or to avoid a greater pain in some future time'. Smith calls the union of these two virtues 'prudence'.

Of all the virtues, prudence is the one that is most useful to the individual.[5] But clearly, he says, people who are equitable, active, resolute, and sober, promise prosperity and satisfaction not only for themselves, but also to every one connected with them. Equally, the rash, the insolent, the slothful, and the voluptuous, store up misfortune not only for the individuals themselves, but also for all those who have anything to do with them.[6]

The most useful social qualities are 'humanity', 'generosity', and 'public spirit'. They are useful either directly to other people ('humanity' and 'generosity'), or through the contribution they make to the maintenance of the institutions which constitute the pattern of social interaction ('public spirit').

Among these clearly other-regarding or collectivity-oriented attitudes and actions, those nearest the self-regarding end of the continuum are amalgamated by Smith under 'humanity'. Smith's 'humanity' consists in 'the exquisite fellow-feeling' a person entertains for the sufferings and good fortune of others people, resenting injuries to them and rejoicing in their successes.[7]

This tender virtue, fundamental to effective social intercourse, is not one which gives rise to a severe problem of engendering it. Unlike prudence, which though a self-regarding virtue is also a far-sighted one, humanity is a matter of immediate reaction without regard for long-term consequences. Hard cases may make bad law, but it is the hard case that is 'humanity's' concern. Even the most humane of humane actions, in Smith's sense of the word, require 'no self-command, no sense of propriety'. They consist only in doing what sympathy would of its own accord prompt us to do. They are a spontaneous outpouring of fellow-feeling, gratifying the need of the other, as we would wish to have our similar needs immediately gratified, regardless of the remote consequences. We simply put ourselves in the here-and-now into the other's position, and vicariously enjoy the other's present pleasures or present relief of pain. Or we feel with them the anguish of their irremediable sufferings, and share their indignation or hatred towards their oppressors, as if their pleasure and suffering were our own, and as if their oppressor were ours also.

Further along the spectrum in the other-regarding direction is the set of attitudes Smith called 'generosity'. The virtue he so labelled is less closely tied to the basic psychic make-up of the human species, and therefore harder to produce through social experience and deliberate training. It is also easier to destroy or lose. We are never 'generous' (in the meaning he gives to the term) says Smith, except when in some respect we prefer some other person to ourselves. We sacrifice some important interest of our own to the interest of someone else. Magnanimous people consider those opposite interests, their own interest and that of the other person, not in the light in which they naturally appear to themselves, but in that in which they appear to an impartial bystander. Thus the soldier who throws away his life in order to defend that of his officer is not doing so out of sympathy for the officer, by viewing the officer as if he were himself. Quite the contrary. He does it out of recognition that the officer is different from himself. He gives his life because he has adopted the far different and for him far more difficult standpoint of an impartial spectator. From that point of view, and to anybody but himself, Smith says, the soldier acknowledges that his own life is a trifle compared with that of his officer.

The examples he gives of the still more austere and difficult virtue required for 'the greater exertions of public spirit' are also to some extent now historical curiosities.[8] They nevertheless make clear his point about collectivity-orientation:

> When a young officer exposes his life to acquire some inconsiderable addition to the dominions of his sovereign, it is not because the acquisition of the new territory is, to himself, an object more desirable than the preservation of his own life. To him, his own life is of infinitely more value than the conquest of a whole kingdom for the state which he serves. But when he compares the two objects with one another, he does not view it in the light in which they naturally appear to himself, but in that in which they appear to the nation he fights for. To them the success of the war is of the highest importance; the life of a private person of scarce any consequence. ... There is many an honest Englishman, who, in his private station, would be more seriously disturbed by the loss of a guinea, than by the national loss of Minorca, who yet, had it been within in his power to defend that fortress, would have sacrificed his life a thousand times rather than, through his fault, have let it fall into the hands of the enemy.[9]

Therefore, Smith says, if it were possible that a person should grow up to adulthood without experiencing the crucial social relationships that were actually capable of inculcating into him the capacity to take the standpoint of an impartial observer, such a person could never either 'exult from the notion of deserving reward nor tremble from the suspicion of meritorious punishment'. All such sentiments pre-suppose the person's acceptance of the notion of some *other* being who is the natural judge of his moods, thoughts and actions. It is only by sympathy, not with his own feelings or those of another sufferer or beneficiary, but only with an *impartial arbiter* of the conduct of both that he can conceive 'either the triumph of self-applause or the shame of self-condemnation'.[10]

It is essential for the continued existence of a society—the system of rule-bound behaviour—and therefore also of the individuals whose survival depend on the co-operation that the rules guarantee, that what Smith calls 'the spectator within the breast' should be one of the controls on conduct.

All societies, as coherent on-going units, are in a state of change, whether sluggishly and imperceptibly, or rapidly and palpably. The rules governing the way in which they will change, whether spontaneously-developed rules or created rules, whether embodied in traditional customs or in deliberately enacted laws, are always a crucially important component of the rule structure.

The impartial spectator within the breast may lead a population to supplant one form of social organization with another, either using the existing rules or rejecting them. But a society may prove incapable of inculcating this impartial spectator, who judges motives and behaviour from a wider perspective than that of the individual himself, into the personality of a sufficiently high proportion of the continual stream of newcomers to it—its babies, infants, children and youths. Without the impartial spectator in the breast, the being who knows and cares about the public weal, the society will not simply change. It will either collapse or be 'overthrown by strangers'.[11]

Not many years ago the idea that a society could disappear was dismissed by many sociologists in the West as absurd. This was especially the case with the Marxist intelligentsia: societies could only change, and in a process of fundamental conflict they changed from an inferior to a superior form. As distinct from the destructibility of the flesh and the mortality of mere men, women and children, in the nineteenth and twentieth centuries the toughness of the social fabric, for good and ill, had indeed been demonstrated in remarkable ways.

Much of the world lay under the administration of colonial powers. Some were ruled more humanely and with more consent,[12] some more brutally, exploitatively and oppressively. Considering only the stability of their regimes, and not their sins, the colonial powers ruled over durable social systems.

In two world wars millions of soldiers and civilians were killed, the property and cities of the metropolitan powers were destroyed on a large scale, yet the institutions of the societies remained intact, or the interludes of mutiny, revolution, displacement of population, and civil war were relatively brief. (China was the main exception.) Massacres were carried out by disciplined troops, and genocide by an orderly bureaucratic process.[13]

More remarkably still, after both wars material losses and social order were restored within a few years, with the society organized along the lines of either its pre-war social system, or new forms of totalitarianism (after the first world war), or (after the second world war) those laid down by the Soviet, British, or American victors. Bourgeois-democratic, communist, or fascist, the breakdown of the system into long-lasting chaos was not envisaged. There would be only reforming alterations of the status quo or a revolutionary transition from capitalism to communism or, from the opposite point view, a rapid or gradual transition from communism to democratic pluralism.

World history since the mid-1960s has familiarized us much more with the spectacle both of societies breaking down and of populations failing to organize themselves effectively for survival.

British society is fortunate in being very far indeed (probably) from any social apocalypse. The general points made above about the requirements of continuing social co-operation, for evil or benign purposes, and their theoretical and empirical grounds, simply warn against taking such benign social co-operation for granted. They are made only as an antidote against the complacent view that, for social solidarity as such, one set of institutions is just as good, or just as bad, as any other.

In recent years the growth of this latter attitude has been especially vigorous. Most importantly and significantly, it has been propagated with particular assiduity in those areas of life which happen, jointly, to be most directly concerned with the recruitment of newcomers to the society and their treatment so that they will be most likely to play a useful part in it. (Useful, in being able and willing to fend for themselves, and to produce a surplus which is available to those who cannot or will not fend for themselves.)

These are the areas of sexuality, procreation, child-care, child-rearing and those qualities of adult mutual-aid which cannot possibly be purchased for members of a society on a large scale for money. By the beginning of the 1990s the received wisdom had become that the institutions which *normatively* and also to a large extent in practice held these areas together in a tight inter-locking package (lifelong heterosexual socially-certified marriage and sexual partnership and parenthood only within socially-certified marriage) were 'not deteriorating, only changing'.

On any performance or characteristic that can be measured from smallest to largest—any 'continuous variable'—most people are clustered on both sides of the category's average score. The numbers then tail off in one direction to the few who have extremely low scores (a few English adults are under 3 feet tall). The numbers tail off in the other direction to the few who have extremely high scores (a few English adults are over 7 feet tall).

Very frequently one category's bell-shaped curve overlaps with that of another category. Very frequently, indeed, the intra-group dispersion from the lowest to highest scorers is much larger than the difference between the average for the two groups—there is a very large overlap. The average height of the category 'women holding British passports' is lower than that of the category of 'men holding British passports'. There are more women in the 'small stature' tail of the distribution than men, and more men in the 'tall stature' tail than women. The curve showing the number of women of different height is shifted to the low end of the distribution as compared with the men's curve. But the curves overlap very considerably. Many women, that is, are taller than many men. Everyone knows that both things are true. Men are taller than women. But many men are smaller than many women.

This is so obvious that no difficulties ever arise when the matter is discussed. No one ever tries to argue that because there are undoubtedly tall women and short men, this proves that men and women are the same height, though it is quite possible to argue that under modern urban and economic conditions the difference is no longer of much social significance (that is a second, separate, but also an empirical matter).

Yet since the 1960s the first argument has been applied quite recklessly to the characteristics, achievements and experiences in the area of sex, child-care, child-rearing, and adult mutual-aid. It can be shown that children biologically created in any number of technically available ways, and subjected to almost any conceivable sort of parenting can be found who do as well on almost any conceivable criterion as some children born to and brought up by their permanently married biological parents. Therefore (the *non sequitur* runs) families without fathers are 'just as good as' the institution of life-long heterosexual monogamy as the context for procreation and socialization. Or they could be just as good as long as they were given enough money: fatherhood is only a matter of cash. Or they would be just as good if the matrix within which sexual practices, and arrangements for the safely and well-being of the child, had been those created by, say, Danish conditions, not by British economic and social development. Or 'the jury is still out', and we do well to remain neutral and inactive on the question of whether these 'alternative families' do on the average a better job for children brought up in them.

'If Mr. Micawber's creditors will not give him time', said Mrs. Micawber, '*they* must take the consequences.'[14] So the policy of social Micawberism is happily propagated, at the expense of a generation of children or more, that we may ready 'in the case of anything turning up'.

Certainly, the loosening of the package of sex and responsibility for the children who are born because of it has been advantageous to identifiable groups in identifiable ways. The most obvious gainers are those whose predecessors had suffered from the sanctions imposed in order to maintain the institutional, normative arrangements holding together sex and child-rearing by both biological parents. (Unmarried children engaging in sexual intercourse, for example.)[15]

But there are other outcomes. There are the other outcomes for children lacking responsible fathers. There are the outcomes for young males who no longer take it for granted that they will become responsible fathers. There are the outcomes, too, for fellow-citizens, which result from the activities of these males who are increasingly both fatherless and free of the expectation that they themselves shall become responsible fathers. In the light of these outcomes, a most surprising thing is that the contentions of adherents of the not-deteriorating-only-changing and the jury-is-still-out schools of thought have been so effective. They have established the powerful impression that all is at least as well as it ever was. They maintain that sex, child-rearing, and the supply of that quality and quantity of adult mutual-aid that cannot be bought and sold with cash, present no more, and probably on balance fewer problems than in the past. Their success is astonishing, for their case flies full in the face not only of common experience. It also flies in the face of every empirical study that has ever been published on the subject that has yielded definite results on the benefits and drawbacks of families with fathers as compared with those households without them.[16]

Notes

1 *The Theory of Moral Sentiments* (1759—sixth ed. 1790), (ed. Raphael D.D., and Mafie, A.L.), Oxford: Clarendon, 1976, p. 187.

2 Judges, 5, 7.

3 The last two classes of action may also be 'egoistic', to the extent that the personal satisfaction derived from 'self-sacrifice' for other persons or for the framework of 'the common good' exceed all other possible personal satisfactions in the situation. However they are labelled (and the first three could be labelled 'egoism type A' and the fourth and fifth 'egoism type B') the two ends of the continuum are distinctly different species of social action.

4 Parsons, T., and Bales, R.F., *Family, Socialization and Interaction Process*, London: Routledge and Kegan Paul, 1956.

5 *Theory of Moral Sentiments*, p. 189.

6 *Ibid.*, p. 187.

7 *Ibid.*, pp. 190-91.

8 An understanding of Smith's examples requires that hostility to their content be held in abeyance, on the grounds that he was bound to take his illustrations from events that the reader in his day could comprehend. Smith clearly has in mind the culture of the eighteenth-century 'gentleman'.

When Smith was writing his *Theory* (he revised it as late as 1790) he was embedded in a society that was producing men who performed remarkable feats of public service, skill, courage, fortitude and achievement (however the remote consequences are judged).

This was true particularly, perhaps, of officers of the Royal Navy (and the craftsmen and common seamen of their crews) in their exploration of the world and the way in which they confronted and overcame the challenges of the sea and contact with strange and potentially hostile societies. The most famous of these officers was James Cook, but there are numerous other examples, such as Vancouver and (not in exploration) Collingwood.

Cook, the son of a Cleveland farm labourer, circumnavigated the globe 1767-71. (Hawkesworth, J., *An Account of the Voyages Undertaken by the Order of his Present Majesty for Making Discoveries in the Southern Hemisphere, and Successively Performed by Commodore Byron, Captain Wallis, Captain Carteret, and Captain Cook*, London: Strahan and Cadell, 1773.) Cook set sail on his last voyage to find the North-West Passage in the year Smith's *Wealth of Nations* was published (1776). The names of his ships are themselves a commentary on the values of the time, the *Endeavour* and the *Resolution*.

Vancouver, after the *Discovery's* strenuous exploration of the Canadian west coast, died at the age of forty, worn out 'in the service of his country'. (Vancouver, G., *A Voyage of Discovery to the North Pacific Ocean*, 1798.) Collingwood's legs literally withered at sea due to his determination, also, to do his duty to 'his country'.

Cook's monument is visible from all over Teesside, and Collingwood's monument at the mouth of the Tyne is visible from far along the coast. When going to sea was still a common aspiration and achievement, both men were held up almost without question as notable cultural exemplars of 'manhood' to North-East boys. It would be an exaggeration to say, however, that for the young the last 30 years can be summed up as progress from Captain Cook to Captain Birdseye.

9   *Theory of Moral Sentiments*, pp. 191-92.

10 *Ibid.*, p. 192.

11 Isaiah, 1, 7.

12 In the Sudan the elite corps of British administrators known as the Sudan Political Service (SPS) never exceeded four hundred British officers (and rarely exceeded 120 on the ground) in the whole fifty-six years of its existence. The SPS, many of them blues from England's elite universities ('the land of blacks rules by blues'), ruled with a high degree of consent a territory nearly four times the area of Texas. A Sudanese scholar judged that 'never has such a splendid selection of men been assembled to do a single job in any part of the world'. (Nigumi, M.A., *A Great Trusteeship*, London: 1958. Quoted in Kirk-Greene, A.H.M., *The Sudan Political Service: A Preliminary Profile*, Oxford: 1982, p. 23.) Dame Margery Perham, a leading academic authority on colonial administration, wrote after visiting the Sudan in 1936 that the District Commissioner was one of the 'supreme types' produced by British culture. (Perham, M., 'Introduction' to

Henderson, K.D.D., *The Making of the Modern Sudan*, London: 1953, xiii. Quoted, *ibid*.) Our thanks are due to the distinguished Sudan specialist, Dr. Ahmed Al Shahi, for drawing our attention to this material.

13 Again, clearly, we are considering only why, prior to the 1960s, the indestructibility of social order was taken for granted among many Western academics, not least among the revolutionary intelligentsia. That the holocaust was among the greatest atrocities, if not the greatest atrocity ever committed in the history of the world is a truth that does not require to be restated here.

14 Dickens, C., *David Copperfield* (1849-50), Harmondsworth: Penguin, 1966, p. 213.

15 Frank Wedekind's famous tragedy of childhood sex, *Frühlings Erwachen* ('Spring's awakening') was published in 1891 but because of censorship left unstaged for another twenty years. It depicted adolescent school children suffering from the sexual repression of the time, talking about their sexual fantasies and orgasms. Fourteen-year-old Wendla is made pregnant by her school friend. The play attacks the society which, without comfort or tenderness, persecutes these innocent children, leaving them and their friends dead or tormented.

When the play was put on by a company of university students of German early in 1992, before an audience mainly of seventeen to eighteen-year-old A-level students, neither the actors nor audience seemed able to take its message seriously to the slightest degree. The play was acted as farce, and the most surprising lines and scenes were received with gusts of laughter. People's sense of humour is a good guide to their social values. Clearly, the problems that confronted Wendla Bergmann, Melchior Gabor, and Moritz Stiefel have never confronted the people concerned, and it appears that they do not have the capacity to comprehend that kind of situation or the tragedies that stemmed from it, much less suffer from them.

16 We would be very grateful to have our attention drawn to any study that contradicts what, given the content of so many of the discussions on the subject, must seem an astonishingly bold remark.

4

The Evidence: Growing Up in the Late Nineteen Sixties

The 1960s saw the beginning of a period of rapid and far-reaching change in the interconnected set of formal and informal social arrangements (a) for controlling who could bring children into the world; (b) for fixing responsibilities for rearing the children, in terms of physique, character and social adjustment; (c) that defined in terms of partners and activities the sources and saliency of sexual pleasure; and (d) that aimed at ensuring so far as possible that each adult had a life-long source of mutual assistance.

Heterosexual adult companionship was always and has increasingly become a desideratum. But to place companionship with one other person at the centre of adulthood under the pre-1960s system was still regarded (perhaps especially among working-class women) as a sign of an inappropriate translation into real life of romantic notions whose place lay in adolescence and in the useful fantasies of cinema and novelette. Marriage, realistically, was child-centred, not spouse-centred. If you did not 'get on' with your wife or husband, then so far as possible you spent your time outside of one another's company. Each could remain an important supplier to the other of practical services, especially in sickness and old age.

To give to sexual excitation a high priority at all (much less to regard it as a right to be sought by whatever self-, mutually- or mechanically-induced means) was regarded as a more-or-less serious weakness or vice.[1]

Sexual exclusivity was a major bulwark against the spread of venereal diseases.[2] The most feared of these was syphilis, with its drastic effects on the child. By the beginning of the 1960s medicine had greatly reduced the dangers. Pragmatically and successfully, venereal diseases were treated without moral criticism *in the clinics*. But generally felt and expressed abhorrence continued to control the behaviour of those who might be tempted to imitate the now more relaxed perpetrators.

Prior to marriage the imperfect intuitions of kin, and people in the other social networks of the couple, gave the signal that 'this has a good chance of succeeding as a stable partnership for child rearing and companionship'. The rough wisdom of general experience of differences in temperament and life-style warned one or other of the risks he or she was running of emotional and other difficulties in the future.[3]

These institutions were guarded not only by newspaper editors, schoolteachers and clergymen. They were protected as a matter of course by members of the public, from hotel receptionists to bank and building society managers.[4] They were protected by mothers and fathers, who sometimes made a harsh and cruel example even of their own daughters. It being difficult to control the transitory and concealed activities at the point of conception, and the connection between the child and the father never being obvious, control fell fiercely on the woman if and when the long-term results became visible to all, to discourage the others.

But even among those whose sense of outraged justice or whose focused sympathy made them insist that the plight of the unmarried mother must not be callously and unimaginatively ignored, much less exacerbated, the balance of their effective opinion still came down against ameliorative measures that would undermine the system. For one of the precise purposes of the system was to minimize the numbers of girls who would otherwise find themselves, with or without their own consent and foresight, being put into that plight by men. Much pain came from breaking the rule; pain to many more would come from weakening it.

The change in public opinion which accompanied the change in these arrangements had depended upon forecasts and hopes that old problems would be diminished, and old and new benefits expanded. At its most idealistic, as the residue of the nineteenth-century belief in progress, there was the notion that all are moving onward and upward in 'the great march of the intellect'[5] and morality. The family could now pass beyond the legalism of binding obligations, out of the confines of claim and counter-claim, without loss, into the realm of life-affirming fellowship. Thirty years after his death, D. H. Lawrence's views began to gain wide acceptance in law and practice: that the existing forms were 'old, dull and dead'.

Like much else that stemmed from the inventiveness of the 1960s, the changes provided copybook examples of a staple of sociological discussion—the unforeseen and unwanted conse-quences of purposive social action. Pornography (to take a conspicuous but far from the most important example) had been generally considered a degraded and infantile interest. Depend-ing on the existence of sexual taboos, pornography would wither as the taboos faded. Instead, pornography extended itself into the everyday life of the general public, making voyeurism an almost unavoidable adjunct of entertainment. But instead of its growth being regarded as a deterioration in public sensibilities, outside certain feminist circles it became normal to regard it as a harmless or even therapeutic feature of the society.

Similarly, very few of those pragmatic reformers who attacked the then existing legal institutions and social usages governing procreation, child-rearing, life-long cross-sex companionship, and life-long mutual assistance had argued that what was then called illegitimacy would—still less should—become commonplace. The two or three generations preceding that of the 1960s had generally agreed that, in Swift's words, nothing could be more unjust than for men 'in subservience to their own appetites, to bring children into the world, and leave the burthen of support-ing them on the public'. In that respect if in few others their attitudes to the family system resembled those of the Lilliputians. It was only as it did become commonplace that assertions appeared with increasing frequency that there were no significant adverse consequences. It was now claimed that empirically there were no important consequences for mother or child resulting from the father not being in effect 'licensed'[6] by society to get children by one particular woman. There were none for the mother or child from the father not committing himself publicly to long-term responsibility for his family, under pain of public disesteem or worse.

When this transformation in custom and law was in its early stages, Eileen Crellin and her colleagues ('Crellin') were able to study at the National Children's Bureau the differences between seven-year-old children whose fathers through formal marriage had publicly committed themselves to the long-term care of their children, and children whose fathers had not done so. (The latter are referred to here for brevity as the 'uncommitted' fathers, but always and only in the sense of the *publicly*-uncommitted fathers. Obviously some fathers married to the mother when their child was born are in essence uncommitted, and some unmarried fathers selflessly devoted to their children.)

All the 17,000 children born in England, Scotland and Wales in the week 3-9 March 1958 were (and are) the subject of periodic follow-up investigations by the National Child Development Study. Of these children, 600 were born outside of marriage. A principal author of the Crellin study of these (as they were called) 'illegitimate' children was Dr M.L. Kellmer Pringle, well-known for her publications on child development.

What were the statistical associations between, on the one hand, birth taking place without the mother being married to the father (a central prohibition of the pre-1960s system) and, on the other, various aspects of the circumstances and personal characteristics of the mother and child?[7]

In Crellin's population, the proportions of the children of married and uncommitted fathers were spread evenly through the social classes. Whereas uncommitted fatherhood had in the past been associated with low social class, by the later-1960s this was no longer the case.[8]

Her findings confirmed that the rapid acceleration in the rise in the frequency of uncommitted fatherhood was not the result of the emergence of an 'underclass' which was repudiating the values of respectable society. Attitudes, law and conduct had been transformed within a decade. No underclass has at its disposal the means of moulding public opinion to achieve such a thing.[9]

It was a change throughout society of the evaluation of what respectable behaviour was. Those changes were being effected by members of society who had access to the means for communicating what is going to be accepted as true and virtuous—the effective intelligentsia. Some members of this part of the intelligentsia certainly adopted, advertised and approved their own elitist and originally insulting version of 'working-class culture'; insulting because the anti-familial, individualistic conduct (hardly cultural conduct) attributed to the working class was precisely that most feared and despised by the respectable working class. They knew only too well and at first hand its consequences under their conditions of life. Only in that extremely attenuated sense was it at any time a question of underclass morality.

Lying behind the changes in the morality of reproduction was the emergence in the U.S.A. and western Europe of a more autonomous youth culture, the individualistic hedonism of which stemmed partly from affluence, partly from anti-war and anti-racist sentiments, and partly from the fear or affectation that the world was on the eve of destruction.

In remoulding attitudes and assumptions about what was factually true and ethically valid, at least as important was a part of the intelligentsia which was largely based in higher education and which made its influence felt most widely through serious newspapers and discussion programmes. Its prime commitment was to draw attention to, and remedy, the evils associated with the system of life-long monogamy. These evils included the subordinated and narrowly domestic life of the woman, the stereotyping of the roles of the son and the daughter at the cost of the latter, and of course in some cases sheer brutality and sexual abuse. Only people who were heartless, who were uncaring, would say anything that could be interpreted in any way as weakening the case for the removal of these evils.

Factual surveys like Crellin's had shown (and continued to show for as long as they were considered worthy to be financed) that on average the life-long socially-certified monogamous family on the pre-1960s pattern was better for children than any one of a variety of alternatives practically applicable to large

urban populations.[10] These surveys undermined aspects of the
arguments put by the defenders of the interests of the various
problem groups. Certain of the righteousness of their respective
causes, there must have been at least a few who consciously
attacked what they suspected might well be true, but inconven-
iently and irrelevantly true. Probably most simply followed the
fashion and unconsciously resisted making themselves familiar
with material damaging to their own confidence and their client-
group's case.

They focused their own and the public's attention on the
problem end of the distribution of the pre-1960s family, and on
the successful end of the distribution of other arrangements for
handling sex, procreation, the physical safety and health of the
baby, child rearing and adult mutual aid. Equipped with an
array of rationalizations which enabled them to sneer at opinions
on the family different from their own ('false consciousness', 'the
social construction of reality', 'the bourgeois problematic', 'moral
panics' and various other terms meaning 'other people's ignorance, ill-will and stupidity') the more articulate and 'better-
informed' elevated themselves above common sense and the
findings of statistical surveys. They demonstrated to their own
satisfaction, and for twenty years to the satisfaction of a complacent academic community and uncritical media of communication, that more or less any opinion other their own was an
ambush set for simpletons by either patriarch or capitalist.
There was no such thing, to use Sir Henry Wotton's old categories, as 'the simple truth' or 'honest thought'.[11] They acknowledged such opinion as suited the interests of their client-
group and cast doubt upon or ignored what they deemed would
be damaging to them. That is, they acted as advocates.

No one who had completed a year's seminars with 150 first-
year undergraduates (most of them females) as one of the
authors did in 1991-92, could doubt that among these opinion-
formers of the near future the pre-1960s family is a thoroughly
discredited set of attitudes and *mores*. Certainly, many asserted
that they were committed to 'the family'. But this was only in the
sense that they wanted one aspect of a successful marriage, a
'loving relationship'—to *be* loved, *on their own terms*. To be pre-

committed 'for a life-time' and 'for better or worse' to render unpaid services to another was an eccentric notion that had never worked in practice, and all they were doing was discarding an oppressive ideology. The only unexpected feature of the seminars was the frequency with which it was assumed or asserted (as a criticism) that the pre-1960s family (as a complicated set of inter-related institutions, not simply as one or other of a number of discrete aspirations) was still the only approved model presented through the influential media.

Yet quite clearly not only had feature programmes led but advertisements had followed in treating the family without fatherhood as acceptable and normal. In Great Britain the citadel of conventional values for the first thirty years or so of its existence was Radio 4 and its earlier equivalents, which continued to bear after his death the stamp of respectability put upon the BBC's whole output by Lord Reith. Within that citadel, 'Woman's Hour' was an inner stronghold of conventional sexual and family morality. By the time these students were complaining about the uniformly family-oriented output of the media, a presenter of 'Woman's Hour' was of the opinion that marriage was an 'insult'. 'Women shouldn't touch it.' In a remark that would have provoked widespread protest from married women only a few years before as an outrageous insult to all of them (and it was indeed condemned by the rare and judicious Barbara Amiel) she wrote that entering the status of spousehood had itself made her 'a legal prostitute'.[12] The popular Cosby Show, a programme portraying family life in a favourable light, was exceptional.

On one occasion the American Vice-President criticised a television comedy. The episode had an audience of 38 million viewers in the United States. He said that it did not help matters when prime TV had the heroine 'mocking the importance of fathers' and her calling her decision to have a baby while unmarried 'just another lifestyle choice'. According to the correspondent of *The Sunday Times* in Washington, Quayle's remarks 'provoked outrage', with editorial writers and talk-show hosts criticising him 'for misunderstanding one of the more intelligent American sitcoms and for a bludgeoning attack on unmarried mothers'.[13]

It has seldom been possible in our researches, even in very substantial and long-term investigations, to assess the effects of social class and income independently of the effects of the commitment of a father. But whenever the data have allowed a tentative assessment, the indication has always been that in each social class, and at each level of income, the commitment of a father, on the measures chosen, has had a significant effect. In all classes the lack of commitment of the father is disadvantageous on the average for the child.

It is plain, and it cannot be imagined to be otherwise, that it is more likely among the poor than among the prosperous that the result of the natural father not being regularly committed over a long period as a member of the child's household will be to the child's disadvantage. As Sir Thomas Browne said of the well-to-do: 'their fortunes do somewhat gild their mischiefs, and their purses compound for their follies'.[14]

The average lower-working-class child whose average father is not there, which is more likely to be the case with the uncommitted than the committed fathers, is much more likely to suffer from material hardship; from irritation and anger from a person who has to cope with him single-handed much of the time; and from the experiences, as he grows up, of living in a flat on a dangerous and unpleasant part of a housing estate.[15]

Crellin allocated the households in her study according to the mother's social class of upbringing (i.e. the mother's father's social class). As the study of unmarried mothers in Scotland carried out by the Scottish Home and Health Department had also reported, there was a striking amount of downward social mobility among the mothers of the children of the uncommitted fathers.[16] This downward mobility started with the employment difficulties faced by the mothers as they neared the time of the birth of, and then gave birth to their child. Some of these difficulties were due to the still considerable stigma that attached to the unmarried mother at the time of the Crellin study. Such difficulties diminish, by definition, when uncommitted fatherhood becomes normal and therefore necessarily socially acceptable, as in the Caribbean.[17] But other difficulties were the consequence of not having the father as the (in principle) sole other full-time contributor to the practical arrangements necessitated by pregnancy and motherhood (whatever the otherwise given supply of assistance from the kin group, the community or the social and educational services).

The characteristics, experiences and achievements of the average child of the married father were markedly different from those of the average child of the uncommitted father. The gradient on almost all measures was first, the adopted children of uncommitted fathers; second, the children of committed fathers; and last, the children of uncommitted fathers.

In the matter of life and death, taking birth order of the child and the mother's young age into account, there was a higher perinatal mortality among the children of uncommitted than committed fathers. The babies of uncommitted fathers were not protected by their mother's class of origin. For among the sample of babies of married fathers there was a tendency for perinatal mortality to decrease the higher the social class, but this was not the case for those of uncommitted fathers.[18] Fifty-two per 1000 children of uncommitted fathers had died by the time they were seven, as against 36 per 1000 of the children of committed fathers.[19]

Twice the proportion of children of the uncommitted fathers had some form of proteinuria, connected with the mother's smoking habits after the twentieth week of pregnancy. (The risk of death was highest of all for the babies of uncommitted fathers whose mothers were smokers.[20]) The proportion of children who died from accidents was also higher among the children of uncommitted fathers.[21]

With regard to physique, at birth the average baby of the uncommitted father weighed less than the baby of the publicly-committed father. Almost twice as many of the former were in the 'low birthweight' category.[22]

The absence of a father who had committed himself to marriage before his child was born was statistically associated with the chances that the mother would be unavailable to the baby and infant during working hours. Only 12 per cent of the women who adopted a child of an uncommitted father went out to work in the child's pre-school years. This was the case with 24 per cent of the mothers who had been married when the child was born. But 61 per cent of the mothers of the non-adopted children of uncommitted fathers had gone out to work in the child's pre-school years. Only 3 per cent of the mothers who had adopted a child had worked full-time in this period of the child's life. Forty-three per cent of the mothers of the children of uncommitted fathers had.

These figures are not a reflection of social class differences. In the group of married parents there is an increase of pre-school working mothers with decreasing social class. There is no such pattern among the other mothers who looked after their own children. Working outside the home before the child was old enough for school was made necessary for the mothers of the children of uncommitted fathers, across the social classes, by economic pressures, reinforced by their own desire for outside company for themselves, and for personal independence.[23]

These mothers were on the average, certainly, worse off than those in the other groups.[24] None of the adoptive mothers were reported as having 'overt' financial problems. The figure for married mothers was 7 per cent. Nevertheless, only 21 per cent of the other mothers had overt financial problems. The fact that 79 per cent did not has be taken into consideration in discussions in which the differences in the experiences and achievements between of children of committed and uncommitted fathers are attributed largely to shortage of money.[25]

The housing experiences and environment of the average uncommitted-father's child are different from those of the average adopted child and the married-parent child.[26]

For good or ill the uncommitted-father's child had a much more mobile existence, changing friends, schools and other familiar things, than either those adopted or those born to a married couple. Twenty per cent of them had moved house at least four times; this was the case with only 7 per cent of the married-parents' children. The most mobile was the child of an uncommitted father who was now in a household where its mother was cohabiting with him: 38 per cent of such children had moved house four or more times.[27]

Only 5 per cent of the uncommitted-fathers' children who were adopted lived in housing conditions of more than 1.5 persons a room. Of those who were not adopted, nearly a quarter lived in these conditions (22 per cent). What is more, the usual tendency for overcrowding to increase with declining social class was absent in the case of the children of uncommitted fathers.[28]

Crellin looked at the child's conditions in terms of the 'basic amenities' at the disposal of its household (indoor w.c., hot water supply, bathroom, cooking facilities). 'In this respect, too, illegitimate children were very much worse off than the legitimate or adopted.'[29] The households of 33 per cent of the first of these groups lacked the use of one of these amenities, 17 per cent of the second group, and only 5 per cent of the third group. In general children in class V households were twelve times more likely than children in middle-class homes (I, II and III non-manual) to live in a household lacking or having to share three or more of these amenities. In the case of the children of uncommitted fathers, the difference was much less marked. Instead of being only a twelfth as likely, the middle-class children in this category were only half as likely as class V children to live without three or more of the household amenities.[30]

At the age of seven the great majority of the children of committed fathers were in the household situation into which they were born, that is, with both their natural parents (90 per cent). Only 27 per cent of the children of uncommitted fathers were with both their natural parents. Forty-six per cent were in other two-parent situations. The rest were scattered into a wide range of household types: 9 per cent were with their own mother only, 7 per cent with their own mother and others, 4 per cent were with a grandparent.

Three per cent were in care.[31] But 11 per cent (as compared with 2 per cent of the total cohort) had been taken into care for longer or shorter periods. In 90 per cent of the cases the first reception into care was before the age of 5. In half the cases the first separation from their home was before they were 18 months old, and in a quarter within their first five months. Of these 38 children, six had been in care almost their entire life. The 38 had experienced 77 receptions into care. The second most frequent cause of being taken into care was the illness of the mother in the absence of a reliable source of assistance to her and the child at home.[32]

The 7-year-olds were assessed on their ability and attainment. Crellin used information from three tests. The first tested the level of their general mental and perceptual development; the second, their reading ability; the third tested their 'arithmetic age'.

The teacher graded each child on its level of general knowledge as 'exceptionally well-informed', 'good background knowledge', 'average', 'below average, rather limited', or 'largely ignorant of the world around it'. Crellin argues that at that age the level of general knowledge is 'to a large extent influenced by the opportunities and stimulation provided for him by his family'.[33]

About the same proportions in each group, adopted, committed-father, and uncommitted-father, were graded 'average' (49 per cent, 49 per cent, 47 per cent).

But only 16 per cent of the adopted children appeared in the below average grades, 28 per cent of the children of the committed fathers, and no fewer than 45 per cent of the children of uncommitted fathers. Only 0.7 per cent of the adopted children were labelled as 'largely ignorant of the world around them', and 4 per cent of the children of the committed fathers, but more than 8 per cent of the children of uncommitted fathers.

At the other end of the scale, 1 per cent of the children of the non-committed fathers were labelled by their teachers 'exceptionally well informed', nearly 3 per cent of the children of committed fathers and over 3 per cent of the adopted children.

On the Southgate reading test, nearly half (49 per cent) of the children of the uncommitted fathers fell into the bottom grade of 'poor'. This was the grade of 28 per cent of the children of committed fathers, and of only 18 per cent of the adopted children.[34] Having a committed father made the second biggest statistical difference after social class: 10 months of reading age—with adoption meaning a further gain of 2 months.

On the test of arithmetical ability especially developed for her study, Crellin found that as usual there was not much difference between the groups of children in the proportions graded as 'average'—about 40 per cent in all three cases. But again, though not so marked as in the reading and general knowledge gradings, there were differences between the groups in the proportions of poor performers and good performers. In the adopted and committed-father groups about 30 per cent scored 7-10 ('good') on the test, but only 20 per cent of the non-committed father group. *Eliminating the effects of social class* and other factors, being the child of a non-committed father made a difference in the statistics of five months in 'arithmetic age'.[35]

Only 3 per cent of the children of committed fathers, but nearly three times that percentage of the children of uncommitted fathers had attended at least three different schools in the first two years of school life. Changing schools means adjusting to different classroom organization, to different standards, to the personalities of different teachers, to different friends. The effects on a child of such high residential mobility are not in all cases detrimental. But 'for children doing badly already ... frequent changes of school are likely to exacerbate further their learning difficulties'.[36]

Mothers were graded on their interest in their children's education. Among those children now in middle-class homes (I, II, and III non-manual) 21 per cent of the mothers of the children of non-committed fathers were classified as showing 'little or no interest'. Only 1 per cent of the adoptive mothers were put in this grade, and 4 per cent of the mothers of children with committed fathers. Only 4 per cent of the class IV adoptive mothers were graded as uninterested, 20 per cent of the committed-father group, and 27 per cent of the uncommitted-father group.[37]

In all aspects of ability and attainment examined by Crellin, the non-committed father group did significantly less well than either the committed-father or adopted groups.

The study carried out on these children in 1966 found that, in general, living in any situation other than being brought up by adoptive or by both of their own parents brought a lower level of educational attainment.[38] It had therefore been expected that those children of uncommitted fathers who were living with their natural parents would perform better than all the other subgroups in the uncommitted-father category. 'If anything the opposite was true.' The *lowest* scores were obtained by children of non-committed fathers who were living with their natural parents.[39] Using D.H. Stott's Bristol Social Adjustment Guides the behaviour of the children was assessed.[40] The proportion of children found 'maladjusted' among the non-committed father sample was much higher than among the other two groups. About two-thirds of both the committed-father and the adopted groups were 'stable' on Stott's test. This was true of under a half of the uncommitted father group. The slightly higher proportion of the adopted than of the committed-father group who were 'maladjusted' was one of the few cases where the gradient adopted/committed-father did not appear (here, 16 per cent, 13 per cent). But a quarter of the children of the uncommitted fathers were 'maladjusted', placing them in their invariable location in the gradient.

Though 'social-class composition' did of course have its own diffuse effects overall, *within each class* the non-committed-father group contained a higher proportion of maladjusted children. The differences between the groups cannot be explained by sex differences. 'If anything, this should have worked in the opposite direction from that found.'[41]

At the time when pressures for change were building up, Crellin's findings between marriage and the child's life-chances reproduced those of other studies and the assumptions of the common sense of the time. The advocates and passive condoners of change could not contradict the findings. They therefore either did not consult or refer to them, or they interpreted them in new ways.

An important body of thought had emerged as part of the general demand for reform. In the large areas of race and gender, problems were now attributed principally to prejudice and discrimination. Prejudice's little sisters, 'stigma' and 'labelling', were immediately available for the purposes of reinterpretation of Crellin's findings and others like them. For in an intellectual community which was increasingly sensitized to prejudice, labelling found the desired resonance, perhaps all the more so because the connection between the larger and smaller concept was not completely obvious.

With an egregiously small amount of evidence, and that which existed throwing little light on its part as one influence among many, 'labelling' was put forward as the main explanation of all the differences between the children of the committed and uncommitted fathers.

Put in an unqualified form for clarity, the differences were all originally only in the mind of the nurse, the doctor, the teacher, the neighbour, with no basis in fact. The commitment or absence of commitment by the father was not an important factor in the situation at all. It was only, then, the way that the children were treated by these people, on the erroneous assumption that the father's commitment was important, that gave rise to the real differences that were observed. Remove stigma and the problem disappears.

On that foundation an enormous social experiment was permitted to go forward. If the foundation proved faulty the lives of the next (much enlarged) generation of children of uncommitted fathers would be affected in the ways discovered in surveys such as Crellin's. These adverse effects would be mitigated only if the quite speculative hopes were realized, that as the disadvantage in itself of being stigmatized was reduced (as in the 1970s and 1980s it undoubtedly was) then whatever element of other disadvantage traceable to stigma would also be diminished or removed.

One of Crellin's most striking findings is that the children of committed fathers were close to, but in nearly all cases 'below' the *adopted* children of *non-committed* fathers. This confirms the idea that in principle alternatives to the pre-1960s family can be 'successful'. That is not here in question. Adoptive parents are 'good' parents because they are a small group of volunteers who are then subject to a further process of selection and rejection as being suitable for child-rearing or not. The question is rather, which alternatives are now relatively successful, or on reasonable grounds of existing data might be relatively successful *on a large scale*? Existing data do not suggest that uncommitted fatherhood and single-motherhood are institutions of equivalent worth to the average child on any of the criteria that are usually adduced in connection with the assessment of its 'best interests'.

We have not yet come across, and we have not yet succeeded in being directed to, any serious statistical study that shows that on the average babies who have lacked a sociological father fare better as babies who have had an effective sociological father. A handful of studies show that on certain criteria there is no difference. But nearly all the serious statistical studies we have examined show that, on the criteria chosen by the study as showing 'better' and 'poorer' ability, performance or achievement (with very few exceptions on individual items), they do worse. The longer the same father has been part of the child's life, and the more effectively the father has taken part in the life of the family, the better the results for the child.

As a current sociological phenomenon, it interesting that so much discussion is directed to, as we might term it, plausibly 'explaining away' the findings that show that across the board, physical weight, height, educational achievements, criminality, life and death itself, are on average connected with the presence or absence of a committed father.

A frequent argument is that the differentials are there, but they are not due to the absence of the father 'as such'. They are due to the absence of money. But the shortage of money is itself due to the absence of the father. And, here again, a gamble was made with the lives of future generations of children on the basis of purely speculative and necessarily political wishes.

Let us assume that it is true that all or a large component of the differentials between fatherless children and children with fathers is due to lack of income and could indeed been counteracted by changes in policy regarding the provision of State benefits for fatherless children and husbandless mothers. It was bold indeed to assume that for that reason State policy would be rapidly changed to accommodate itself to these needs.

In the event, the same public opinion which was not simply increasingly sympathetic to plight of the lone mother, but also increasingly perceived it as the normal, acceptable state of affairs, showed itself surprisingly reluctant in election after election to vote into national government the party which promised most in terms of improved State benefits. In the meantime Hegel's words operated on the children of lone mothers with full force: philosophy bakes nobody's bread.

Furthermore, if the differences in criminality, mother's interest in the child's schooling and so forth are accepted as data, then we know of no studies that do support the view that money has that dominating role in the rearing of children. On basis of general theoretical and empirical work in sociology and psychology it is implausible. Of course money makes some difference to some things; we have already emphasized that above. It is highly likely to make an important and valuable difference in physical health in one way or another. It is obvious that the state of single-parenthood drives a poor mother into all sorts of difficulties. She is short of money; she needs to work; she is unable to pay for substitute child care; the child is ill and she must jeopardize her job to look after it; and so on into an ever descending spiral of financial and emotional distress.

But in the sociological and psychological aspects of child-rearing there are no studies in social policy that we have seen which show anything that suggests that for every £50 or £100 of extra weekly income for children whose fathers are absent or present and do not 'father', there is a demonstrable reduction in the differentials. (Any actual study would be not be so crude, but it would require something of this nature.) What effect has any given amount of money on the likelihood that the mother will visit an antenatal clinic; on the likelihood that the mother will smoke into the last months of her pregnancy; on the likelihood that she will take an interest in the child's schooling, and on the likelihood that the child will perform at a certain level at school?

We have not considered the strictly social-policy question of what the consequences would be—if this degree of importance of money in child rearing could be shown—of it being drawn from the social security budget. But it seems obvious to laymen in these matters that it would be difficult to give 'fatherless' families as defined in some bureaucratically necessary way an extra £100 a week without giving an extra £100 a week also to every other category of claimant.

This would be an attractive way of surreptitiously making old age pensioners and the unemployed better off, and generally making the distribution of income more equal in the society. But on the specific point of the effect for the better on at any rate a wide range of the characteristics and experiences of fatherless children, we have yet to see any evidence.

It takes time for children to grow up and show the consequences, if any, of one family background rather than another. It takes resources to set up a cohort study. We are therefore dependent, even in the latest volumes, on reports of family experiences in the more or less distant past. It is then possible to argue without the fear of evidential contradiction that the children born recently will not show in five or ten or fifteen years time the same average differentials as appeared in the evidence about their predecessors—because there has been a reduction in the stigma attached to being brought up in a family where there is no father; because the damage from divorce will be less, now that it need not be preceded by quarrels; because services and benefits are now improved and will be further improved, and so on.

Everyday experience and culturally-defined 'common sense' have often been overturned as mere superstition by scientific inquiry: that statement probably summarizes as well as any other the reason for the successes of urban-industrial societies. On the other hand, 'a science with more than six variables is an art'. It has therefore become possible at one and the same time to deny that wisdom lies in common sense and—without any contrary evidence being available or presented—deny that the available scientific data are valid. Given the nature of the dominant media of communication, people with a reasonable amount of sophistication and a personal interest, or with a selfless interest in the plight of their chosen group, or a devotion to a righteous cause, can now argue away *both* common sense *and* the only available statistical evidence. They can baldly and briefly assert that both common sense and statistics are inferior to their own version of what is factually correct and ethically right. Their feeling of moral rectitude enables them to say, with Wordsworth,

> Here then we rest; not fearing for our creed
> The worst that human reasoning can achieve
> To unsettle or perplex it.

Elitism can be pushed no further. The result is that along with common sense any set of figures now, and any conceivable set of figures that could be produced at whatever expense and with whatsoever skill in the future, can be plausibly denounced. Too much confidence should not be put, therefore, in the contribution that decisive statistics can make to rallying support for a necessary public policy.[42]

Notes

1 The relationships of a Harold Nicholson and a Vita Sackville-West, each to members of their own sex, and their emotional dependence on each other in the 1930s was to respectable working-class people very much the behaviour of a *decadent* upper class.

2 There is approximately a 1:6 chance of a mother passing on the HIV virus to her child. Only two of 3,800 pregnant women tested in 1988 at St. Thomas' hospital, London, were HIV positive; in 1990 18 of 4,100 pregnant women were HIV positive. At St. George's hospital, London, 11 of 4,000 pregnant women were HIV positive; four years previously none of the 3,000 pregnant women tested there had been HIV positive. *Lancet*, 17 May 1991. The first report on the chief medical officer of health's study of blood samples from 27 ante-natal clinics and six sexual-diseases clinics showed that 1:500 pregnant women in inner London were HIV positive, and in West Lambeth 1:200 (11 out of 2,000), while remaining still very rare outside London. *The Times*, 18 May 1991.

3 An anomaly of the 'left' and 'right' divide in politics and social-welfare policy is that the left, which is usually the exponent of 'accountability', 'community', and the wisdom that resides in 'the people', discounts out of existence the value of these processes here. Sex, procreation, child-rearing are the private affair of each single individual. Anyone else whomsoever can properly be brusquely dismissed with a 'Mind your own business!'

4 When Jerry Lee Lewis, the American rock-and-roll star, visited England for a tour in the late 1950s, revelations about his 'scandalous' sex life led not only to his hotel bookings, but all his shows being cancelled.

5 Keats was confident that there was proof that 'Providence subdues the mightiest minds to the service of the time, whether it be in Knowledge or Religion'. Keats on Wordsworth, in a letter to J.H. Reynolds, 3 May 1819.

6   One of the few sources to which the author was eventually directed as showing that there is no difference in the average success of one set of arrangements for rearing children as against a wide variety of other arrangements is Hugh Lafollette, 'Licensing Parents', *Philosophy and Public Affairs*, 9, 2, 1980. This is presumably because his argument depends upon the proposition that life-long monogamous couples, fastened into the relationship by law and public opinion, could and very often did cause great harm to their children (as well as to each other and third parties). But who ever said otherwise? The rules of courting, engagement and marriage were precisely a recognition of the fact that people who meet in rapture may part in agony, i.e. they were themselves a system of informal licensing. The issue is: in terms of *specified results*, on the basis of *any data we at present have*, has one system worked significantly better than others *on the distributional average*?

7   Crellin, E., Kellmer Pringle M.L., and West, P., *Born Illegitimate: Social and Economic Implications*, Windsor, England: NFER, 1971.

8   *Ibid.*, p. 39. Classes I and II contributed 16 per cent to the population of illegitimate children studied, the non-manual class III 5 per cent, the manual class III 33 per cent, classes IV and V 27 per cent, and class not given 20 per cent. The lone mothers themselves, however, clearly fall into a lower class, as measured by educational standards.

Highest qualification of head of household
Great Britain, 1988 and 1989 combined:-

lone parent households

degree or equivalent	2%
higher ed., not degree	6%
GCE 'A' level or equiv.	7%
GCE 'O' level or equiv.	23%
no ed. quals.	45%

other households with dependent children

degree or equivalent	13%
higher ed., not degree	14%
GCE 'A' level or equiv.	13%
GCE 'O' level or equiv.	15%
no ed. quals.	18%

General Household Survey No. 20, 1989, London: HMSO, 1991.

9   Anthony Heath found, from the surveys he reviewed, that there was not a different set of inculcated and socially-sanctioned *values* of the permanently-unemployed poor. (Heath, A., in *Understanding the Underclass*, London: Policy Studies Institute, 1992.)

10　That had yet proved viable for large populations, as distinct from carefully pre-selected or self-selected small groups, for example, successful foster or adoptive parents of all backgrounds and tendencies (though these are predominantly themselves socially-certified monogamous couples), Kibbutzim, and so forth.

11　How happy is he born or taught
That serveth not another's will,
Whose armour is his honest thought,
And simple truth his only skill.

This man is freed from servile bands
Of hope to rise or fear to fall;
Lord of himself, though not of lands,
And having nothing, yet hath all.

Sir Henry Wotton, 'The True Gentleman', 1530.

12　Murray, J., *Options*, July 1992, p. 8. Amiel's pre-view comments are to be found in 'Flat Earth Woman Broadcasts Her Woes', *The Sunday Times*, 14 June 1992.

13　'Quayle Shoots from the Lip as Bush Flounders', *The Sunday Times*, 24 May 1992. Quayle accordingly reversed his position: lone-mothers were all modern 'heroines'.

14　Sir Thomas Browne, *Religio Medici* (1643), New York: Oxford University Press, 1972, p. 64.

15　Dangerous and unpleasant parts of housing estates came out of the same social and intellectual climate, and frequently from the same people who thought then and insist now that there is no difference for the child between the family where there is a committed father and the family where there is not a committed father. The only difference is that boarded-up windows, graffiti on the walls, tenants in constant fear, and in many cases 'the final argument of kings', dynamite, are dramatic and undeniable results. By contrast, the damage to the child from not having a committed father is an average occurrence, hidden from sight in the contestable mysteries of statistical tables.

16　Weir, S., *A Study of Unmarried Mothers and their Children in Scotland*, Edinburgh: Scottish Home and Health Department, 1970.

17　Rodman, H., 'The Lower Class Value Stretch', *Social Forces*, 42, 1963; Rodman, H., 'Illegitimacy in the Caribbean Social Structure: A Reconsideration', *American Sociological Review*, 31, 5, 1966.

18　Crellin and others, p. 54 and p. 143.

19　*Ibid.*, p. 53.

20　*Ibid.*, p. 55.

50

21 *Ibid.*, p. 68.

22 *Ibid.*, p.47.

23 *Ibid.*, p. 61.

24 Health visitors noted whether or not financial problems were evident in the family, *ibid.*, p. 65.

25 *Ibid.*, p. 155.

26 The General Household Survey, 1989, gives the housing profile of ownership status of lone-parent households as compared with other households with dependent children:

Tenure of lone parents with dependent children

owner occupier, owned outright	7%
owner occupier, with mortgage	28%
rented from local authority or new town	54%
rented privately, or from Housing Association or co-op, unfurnished	8%
rented privately furnished	2%
rented with job or business	1%

Tenure of other households with dependent children

owner occupier, owned outright	6%
owner occupier, with mortgage	70%
rented from local authority or new town	17%
rented privately, or from Housing Association or co-op, unfurnished	3%
rented privately furnished	1%
rented with job or business	3%

27 Crellin and others, p. 68.

28 *Ibid.*, p. 64.

29 *Ibid.*, p. 64.

30 *Ibid.*, p. 65.

31 Numerous reports on the failures of institutional care cast doubt upon the feasibility of replacing the pre-1960s family with *widespread* communal provision for child-rearing as a normal replacement for care by the biological parents—in effect, putting a much higher proportion of children 'into care'. See, for example, Levy, A., and Kahan, B., *The Pin Down Experience and the Protection of Children*, Stafford: Staffordshire County Libraries, 1991; Social Services Inspectorate, *A Report of an Inspection of Residential Child Care in the Borough of Sunderland*, Gateshead: Social Services Inspectorate, Northern Region, 1992.

32 Crellin and others, p. 66.

33 *Ibid.*, p. 74.

34 *Ibid.*, p. 160.

35 *Ibid.*, p. 161. In her analysis of variance, main effects model, Crellin examined the separate effects of social class, legitimacy status, family size, sex, and birthweight. 'In summary, the [non-adopted] illegitimate children's performance remains the worst, even allowing for the effect of a number of social factors.' p. 83.

36 *Ibid.*, p. 83.

37 *Ibid.* p. 84.

38 Pringle, M.L.K., Butler, N.R., and Davie, R., *11,000 Seven-year-olds*, London: Longman, 1966.

39 Crellin and others, p. 86.

40 Stott, D.H., *The Social Adjustment of Children: Manual to the Bristol Social Adjustment Guides*, 3rd edn., London: ULP, 1966.

41 Crellin and others, pp. 90-91.

42 Especially when the main medium of communication and persuasion is television, it must be true that, as compared with the person with an academic argument suited to the long lecture and the day's seminar, the person with a passionate slogan and a hard case is more interesting. He is also much easier to accommodate within the format of a 'discussion' that by its nature as a vehicle of entertainment (even when it is also being most seriously instructive). Ordinary television can cope with nothing much more technical than percentages, and with not too many of them. Its normal diet is 'sound bites'. It feeds on short bursts of catchy phraseology that fit neatly into the programme maker's preconceived mosaic. In the battle for public opinion, that is, the media strongly favour the pressure groups acting on behalf of the special interests of one-parent families in higher state benefits and reduced public stigma.

5

The Evidence: One Thousand Newcastle Children and their Fathers 1947-1980

In 1979-80, under the aegis of the Human Development Unit of the Nuffield Psychology and Psychiatry Department of the University of Newcastle upon Tyne, Professor Israel Kolvin and his colleagues studied 264 men and women. They were a random sample of the babies born in Newcastle upon Tyne in May and June 1947, now aged 32-33. The researchers already had detailed information about all them, as babies, infants and adolescents. Some of the figures given below refer to all these children, not only to those restudied when they were adult.[1]

What statistical association, if any, was there between on the one hand the absence of their fathers, for whatever reason of irresponsible sexual intercourse or divorce, and on the other the lifetime experiences and achievements of these men and women?

The data provided by even the most sophisticated social research are crude in relation to the problems they address. Statistical association in itself does not establish what is loosely termed a 'causal' relationship. What if data from many sources, and statistical analyses of them, do always show an association between A and B? The reason may be that both A and B only ever appear when C is present, the 'cause' of both. If a C factor can be discounted, the question may still remain: does A 'cause' B, or does B 'cause' A?

But if association is constantly shown, at any rate within a particular system (e.g. to a part of British society as it was at various times) then, in spite of all the crudity of the best available research, the possibility that A causes B certainly cannot be discounted. For any one of a variety of reasons, some people want to deny that a particular, regularly repeated statistical association is a true finding. Or, if they find it too implausible to deny any longer that it is a true finding, to deny that it can be a causal relationship. All they can do then is to 'explain away' the data in a more or less elaborate way, without being able to produce any concrete findings which actually contradict those data.

Kolvin and his colleagues ('Kolvin') used the full range of the statistical techniques available to the social sciences in the late 1970s. For brevity and simplicity, reference will be made here only to some of the more striking percentage-point differences, excluding those which, though statistically significant (i.e. the difference was unlikely to an accident of sampling) were small.[2]

The Father and the Home

Kolvin first considered the relationship between fatherhood and the child's experiences generally in its home environment. Were there 'deficiencies in family wellbeing' associated with the absence of a father or with the father, though present, absconding to a greater or less extent from parental care for his family?[3] His criteria included parental illness, poor physical and domestic care of the child (personal and domestic dirtiness, poor clothing), debt, unemployment, overcrowding, and general incompetence on the part of the mother. Marital instability was included as a deficiency. The loss of a father through death was not included.

These and other deficiencies were grouped into six categories. Respondents were put into the set of those who suffered none of the six; those who lived in homes with one deficiency or more; and those who lived in homes where there were three or more deficiencies.[4]

In families who were not deprived at all when the child was 15, 83 per cent of the fathers had been present since birth. This held for only 53 per cent in the families suffering multiple deprivation.[5] The mothers of all of the children in the non-deprived households had a husband when the baby was born in 1947. In the multi-deprived households 17 per cent of the children were the children of publicly-uncommitted fathers.[6] Where the father had not been present for any of the 15 years, the child was three times more likely to be in a family of multiple deprivation than the child whose father had been there for all the 15 years.

Of course, Kolvin says, the father's mere presence throughout childhood does not ensure the existence of qualities which create a home in which the child is given material and emotional support, and where there is a model for direction, guidance and identification. Among the always-present fathers, a strong statistical association appears between the father showing various traits and the child's home being a good one in other respects. Fifty-three per cent of the fathers in the non-deprived families were perceived by the member of the research team making the observation as 'effective, kind and considerate'. Only 7 per cent of the fathers in the multi-deprived families were so rated. On the criterion of 'father's participation in domestic tasks', the majority of the fathers in the multi-deprived group participated poorly (66 per cent). This was the case with very few of the fathers in the non-deprived families (2 per cent).

'In brief, the deprived groups were characterized by the ... absence of fathers and, even when present, these tended to be inadequate providers who made little contribution to domestic activities and were seldom thought to be competent and caring.'[7]

Eliminating the effect of social class as far as the figures allow, and by way of illustration taking only the children in social classes IV and V, the effect of having on Kolvin's criteria a 'good' father can be clearly seen. For example, of the class IV and V children who were originally non-deprived, and remained non-deprived in 1957, 69 per cent had fathers with 'good personality' and 57 per cent had fathers who were 'good providers'. Only 16 per cent of the fathers in this category 'participated poorly in domestic tasks'. There were bad and good fathers in all classes, but bad or good fathering had its effect in each of them.

The Home and the Child

Having shown that there is a statistical association between the conduct of the father and the extent of deprivation in the father's family—which again is mere confirmation of common sense—Kolvin then examines the effects on the child of being brought up in a non-deprived as compared with a multi-deprived family.

The children were weighed at birth and on six other occasions up to the age of 15. At birth there were no significant differences between children in the families where on the Kolvin criteria there was no deprivation as compared with those where there was multi-deprivation. (The difference between the birthweights of the children of committed and uncommitted fathers is a different issue.) But significant differences appeared at the second weighing, and the average weights of the two sets of children widened as they grew up. It was the same with their height. (It is difficult to see how these findings could have been significantly affected by the children being 'labelled' by those conducting the measurements as being from a class V deprived home, a class V non-deprived home, and class I deprived home, a class I non-deprived home, and so on.)

Other adverse personal characteristics also appeared with greater frequency among the children from the multi-deprived households. For example, 37 per cent of them had speech defects by the time they were five, as compared with less than half that proportion in the non-deprived group.[8]

The children from the multi-deprived families were more likely to suffer from accidents than those in the non-deprived group. By the age of five, 65 per cent of the former, as compared with 45 per cent of the latter, had suffered one or more accidents. For example, the multi-deprived children were nearly four times as likely to have been burnt or scalded (23 per cent as compared with 6 per cent).[9]

When they were ten years of age their teachers rated the children on various skills and interests. On every measure the multi-deprived children were given the lowest average rating. For example, on craft ability 41 per cent of the non-deprived were rated highly; only 2 per cent of the multi-deprived were. Here, no doubt labelling did play a part in elevating or depressing the enthusiasm and abilities of all the children, and may well have been decisive in some cases.[10]

The same pattern of differences persisted, not only in the whole range of academic abilities and attitudes at school, but in all aspects of school life. This was true even of sports activities. When they were 15, 45 per cent of the non-deprived children, and less than half that proportion of the multi-deprived (21 per cent) were rated as being interested in games.

Whatever the defects of intelligence tests, different degrees of success in completing them at the age of 11 was an important factor in a child's life. Similarly, whatever the defects of the society in which they lived, scoring highly rather than poorly made it easier to progress within that society on that society's terms. The Newcastle upon Tyne 32-33-year-olds studied in 1980 had been given IQ tests when they were aged 11, in 1958. The mean score of the non-deprived children was four points above the standard for the test; the score for the multi-deprived children was 13 points below. In the arithmetic test the non-deprived children scored 8 points above the standard, the multi-deprived 8 points below. In English there was a gap of 19 points between the two sets of children.

In 1959 they were again tested, using Raven's Progressive Matrices (widely considered to be one of the most culture-free tests available). The pattern of differences was repeated.[11]

When they were 12 and then when they were 14 they were rated on the Mill Hill Vocabulary Scale. The same scale was used again when they were 32-33, in 1980. Among the men the gap between the two groups was now 10 points (a mean score of 103 against one of 93); among the women 7 points (98 as against 91).[12]

If marrying someone who has the ability to score highly in the Mill Hill Vocabulary Test is regarded as preferable, other things being equal, to marrying someone whose score is poor, then the multi-deprived men did badly. The non-deprived men had married women of just below average intelligence. The multi-deprived men had married women whose mean score was nine points below average. (The rated intelligence of the women played no part in their 'success' in finding intelligent partners: the women in both groups found husbands of average intelligence (101; 100).)[13]

By 1980, of the men who had been in multi-deprived families when they were children of five, 51 per cent had criminal records. This was more than four times the figure for the non-deprived males (12 per cent). Fifteen per cent of the multi-deprived men had been convicted at least eleven times, and had been incarcerated for an average of 21 months. By comparison, only 2 per cent of the non-deprived men had as many as eleven convictions or more, and they had been incarcerated on the average for 8 months.[14]

If the term is preferred, the otherwise multi-deprived were also much more frequently 'labelled' as law breakers. Law-breakers or not, for the children and adults concerned a police record was not an advantage in society as it was constituted at that time. If law-breakers, however admirable that made them in the eyes of those who see criminals as rebels against intolerable injustices and so on, months in prison were unlikely to have been regarded by most of the multi-deprived prisoners themselves as the way they would have chosen to plan their lives or spend their time, even in the cause of social disruption.

The Father as a Protective Factor in Deprived Homes

The fathers' characteristics had been described in 1962 when the study team had known the families for 15 years. Of men who by 1980 had still avoided being labelled as offenders, 48 per cent had fathers who had been described as 'effective and kind'. Of those who did come to be labelled as offenders, only 20 per cent had fathers who had been so described.[15]

Kolvin looked particularly at the fathers of boys and girls from deprived homes only, thus isolating the effect of the father, to the extent made possible by the data available in the study.

Among deprived males, one of the six most important factors he isolated as protection against ever (to the age of 33) being labelled as a delinquent was the 'effective personality' of the father. Among the non-delinquent deprived males 26 per cent, but among the delinquent deprived males only 14 per cent had such fathers.[16]

He found that the presence of the natural father was one of the four most powerful protectors against delinquency among the girls.[17] When they were 10 years of age, the natural father was still present in the families of 61 per cent of the girls who came to be labelled as delinquents. By contrast, he was still present in the families of 81 per cent of those who, in spite of coming from deprived families, had not to the age of 33 ever been labelled as delinquents.[18]

It need hardly be said that these statistics deal with differences between *the averages of groups*. Where there was deprivation and poor fathering the deficit was sometimes capable of being remedied, and such deficits were sometimes compensated for in benign environments of kin, neighbourhood, or school. Some children in the unfathered or poorly-fathered group scored highly in intelligence tests, were keen on sport, and were never in trouble with the police. Some of the children in the well-fathered group scored poorly, were rated as apathetic, had criminal records and so on. It would therefore have been pure prejudice to conclude from the fact that a particular child was a member of one group or the other that he or she was either good or bad at school, was either a shoplifter or not. But it is pure obscurantism to deny that the *statistical chances* of children being physically smaller, stammering, being poor scorers in intelligence tests, or having a criminal record, depended greatly on their home background; and the quality of their home background, at the time and place of the Newcastle 1000 studies, depended greatly on the father.

Notes

1   Kolvin, I., Miller, F.J.W., Scott, D. McI., Gatzanis, S.R.M., and Fleeting, M., *Continuities in Deprivation?: The Newcastle 1000 Family Study*, Aldershot: Avebury, 1990.
      Miller, F.J.W., Court, S.D.M., Knox, E.G. and Brandon, S., *The School Years in Newcastle upon Tyne*, London: OUP, 1974.
      Miller, F.J.W., Court, S.D.M., Walton, W.S. and Knox, E.G., *Growing Up in Newcastle upon Tyne*, London: OUP, 1960.
      Spence, J.C., Walton, W.S., Miller, F.J.W. and Court, S.D.M., *A Thousand Families in Newcastle upon Tyne*, London: OUP, 1954.

2   The principal component and other statistical analyses, detailing the relationship between deprivation, the role of the father in the child's life, and the social class of the family, are partly detailed in the published volume. Most of them, however, are available on request from the authors. (See Kolvin and others 1990, pp. 376-7.)

3   A defect of the Kolvin figures is that certain aspects of bad fathering are included among the criteria of deprivation themselves. 'Deprivation of parental care ... could be temporary or partial, or permanent by separation ... and could affect one or both parents. It included disruption of the family by ... desertion or divorce, by illness or parental work', *ibid.*, pp. 11-12. It

looks as if the importance of the father's presence and conduct became increasingly apparent as the data came to be analysed; by then the researchers simply had to make the best use possible of the material provided from the study as originally designed.

4   Kolvin and others, p. 18.

5   *Ibid.*, p. 41.

6   *Ibid.*, p. 37.

7   *Ibid.*, p. 41.

8   *Ibid.*, pp. 105-6.

9   *Ibid.*, p. 105.

10   'Labelling', especially in criminology and the sociology of education, has been given prominence as the cause of a person's attitudes, activities and achievements. According to this view, teacher expectations towards children from broken homes largely explains their poor school performance (see e.g. Mortimer, J., and Blackstone, T., *Disadvantage and Education: Final Report to the Joint Working Party on Transmitted Deprivation 1980*, London: Heinemann, 1982).

11   Kolvin and others, pp. 109-10.

12   *Ibid.*, p. 124. The argument has been increasingly put in the past ten years that in the link between educational failure and atypical family circumstances the mechanism is largely economic (e.g. Lambert, L., and Streather, J., *Children in Changing Families*, London: Macmillan, 1980). Each and all of the father's activities could similarly be subtracted and the same unhelpful argument put, that it is not 'really' the absence of the father, but the absence of the activity. If in the concrete case—as distinct from some theoretical possibility that the activity could or ought to be performed by someone else—the activity is absent because the father is absent, then the problem is the absence of the father. This applies even if the very dubious argument is accepted that 'economic' factors are as salient as suggested.

13   Kolvin and others, p. 124.

14   *Ibid.*, p. 278.

15   Miller, F.J.W., Court, S.D.M., Knox, E.G. and Brandon, S., *The School Years in Newcastle upon Tyne*, London: OUP, 1974. Kolvin and others 1990, pp. 279-80.

16   Kolvin and others 1990, p. 278.

17   *Ibid.*, p. 289.

18   *Ibid.*, p. 287.

6

What's Left and Right in Childrearing, Sex and Face-to-Face Mutual Aid?

In the case of the figures on crime, the emphasis until recently has been on denying that they really show an increase. The principal exponents of the view that crime has or may have risen, but if it has this is to be condoned or even applauded (the criminals being prefigurative revolutionaries) have been, and still are, to be found in the so-called New Criminology (see Chapter 7). In the case of the family, since the late 1960s there have been far more commentators who have sought and celebrated the change in family morality and conduct. There has therefore been far less controversy over the overall statistics. They show that enormous changes have taken place within the space of a few years. (A brief reminder of the main figures is contained in the Appendix.)

Why do so many more men as compared with the recent past never undertake to be—or withdraw from being—'fathers' to their biological offspring, i.e. are not present from the moment of the child's conception full time for a life-time in the household of their children?

Secondly, is the father's absence from a position of responsibility for his children[1] of any importance—beyond the obvious effect it has, when he takes no responsibility whatsoever, of making it the duty of other people, through their taxes or voluntary philanthropic work, to look after his children by providing money and other aid to the mother?

The answer to the first question will be found if we understand the profound change that has taken place suddenly and recently in general public attitudes, not only those of absent fathers. How do we now believe we should handle such crucial and difficult matters as (i) sex, (ii) pregnancy and childbirth, (iii) the provision of resources for the care of the baby, and baby care itself, (iv) the rearing experiences the baby should have, to make it into a recognizable and not too troublesome member of its own society, and (v) long-term mutual aid between adults on a face-to-face basis?

With the spread of industry and the growth of great cities, the institutions of most areas of life, led by and then strongly affected by the economy, discarded the use of strongly internalized 'sacred' or quasi-sacred beliefs as a basis for social organization. These 'secularized' institutions experienced a brief period during which their dominant theory was that rational exchange maximized personal welfare throughout the population. But, under the stress of the real experiences of industrial and urban life, social theory was very quickly and strongly affected by the obviously adverse, unintended and unexpected consequences resulting from this system.

England was first on the scene with both the modern factory and the industrial town. She was the first to experience the horrors of life in the textile mill for the pauper apprentices, in the mine for women and tiny children, in the overcrowded and insanitary towns for the victims of cholera and typhus. In some cases these consequences were adverse for one or other of the parties engaged in what that party had thought was a rational voluntary exchange of equivalents (one or all of the parties 'getting more than they'd bargained for'). More importantly there were the drastic adverse effects *on others* of rational exchanges struck for the benefit of the bargainers.

Rational exchange between individuals or associations (the theory of the free market) was quickly made subject to rational law (i.e. state control and state collectivism, approved by certain schools of socialism, but not only by socialists). Rational law would be the instrument which would mitigate these unanticipated and adverse effects on one or all of the bargainers themselves. Much more importantly, it would remove or reduce adverse third-party effects, including third parties as yet unborn i.e. effects from which future generations would suffer.

The family was peculiar in resisting all these developments. It retained its pre-market and pre-statute-law characteristics, being only gradually and slowly modified, into the reign of Edward, the two Georges, and the young Elizabeth II. It retained until well into the second half of the twentieth century, that is, many of the forms and attitudes that had grown up from the very earliest days of English Christianity, when Pope Gregory was first asked for his advice by St. Augustine of Canterbury on sex, marriage, and child rearing (because 'these uncouth people', the English, desperately required guidance on these matters).[2] The Roman Catholic Church not many years ago authoritatively restated its view on the family.[3] We can refer to this type of family as the 'pre-1960s' family; or if we want to emphasize the element of the 'sacred' in the institution, as a firm Jew and a lax Anglican we can impartially call it the 'Catholic' family, in whatever sections of society 'sacred' elements were and are still found.

To say that relationships encompassed within the 'Catholic' family were sacred does not mean that they were arbitrary, and lacked correspondence with secular rule and reflection. They were quite clearly ways of dealing with some of the most powerful forces for good or evil, for solidarity or disruption, in the human psyche. People's propensity to produce children—and society's need for them if the pattern of social co-operation is to survive for more than a single generation—always raises the problem of who is to care for them. It has been historically a reasonable rule (not the only possible one, kinship institutions are very various) that the highly labour intensive activity of child care should be allocated to the biological parents on a very long-term basis.

Procreation before the days of artificial and self-insemination was a matter of sexual intercourse. The powerful drive of sex is peculiar in several ways. Unlike food, where the human daily intake for all men and women, all through life, is 2,500 calories, give or take a 1000, sexual appetites differ enormously among men, among women, between the sexes, and in the course of a lifetime. The rhythms of men and women differ.

One way of reducing dissatisfaction is to conceal from the poorly-endowed the riches they will never be able to enjoy. If the biological parents are to be held together for the long period required for their task of child care and child rearing to be completed, their relationship must not be subject to the strain imposed on it by more satisfactory sources of sexual gratification appearing and attracting one of them away. Historically a reasonable rule has been, therefore, that courting should be a matter for market-type relationships ('shopping around'), but that sexual capabilities should not be allowed to enter into the decisions of the parties (the *rule*—infringed in practice—of premarital virginity of both the man and the woman). The Catholic family had this rule. (In other societies other usages, regarded as devilishly inferior—'ye beastly devices of ye heathen' —have allowed premarital sexual licence.)

When a voluntary choice of partner has been made, then all market-type elements are transcended. The relationship between the man and woman, and all other members of the community towards them, is from then on defined by their status as husband and wife. Two people are originally committed to being, but are in any case are then socially constrained to be, dependable sources of services to their immature children and for a life-time to each other. The *rule* (though not to the same extent the actuality) prevails of life-long sexual exclusivity and fidelity, whether the 'surprise packet' in the transaction, 'sex', turns out to be a good bargain or not. They are no longer related by the modern commercial term 'partner', but by the medieval and sacred term 'holy estate'.

Even today the Roman Catholic Church stresses the 'reasonableness' of these arrangements. The future of humanity passes through the family, so that 'every person of good will', not just the religious Catholic, should recognize their secular merits in coping with the difficult problems to which they are addressed. The Church has learned at the school of Christ, certainly, but also at 'the school of history'. They are sacred arrangements, but they correspond to human welfare. Complying with the Church's rules of wifehood and husbandhood, of motherhood and fatherhood, is to abide by decrees that are sacred. But they are not on

that account either arbitrary or inscrutable, and they are
certainly not more damaging than alternative systems to either
the person, or to her or his contemporaries, or to posterity.[4]

Much more than other organizations not specifically religious,
the Catholic family (in the sense we have given the term above)
retained elements of the sacred, and of *internalized* conceptions
of social duties which the individual required himself or herself,
and other people, to fulfil. Internalization meant that the person
paid the heavy price of 'feeling guilty' if he did not do what had
been internalized as the 'right' thing to do. But it was not only a
matter of personal life-style *even as a dutiful individual*. It
concerned compulsory communal norms, those regarded as being
of the utmost importance to members of a society or association,
the *mores*. The *mores* are views of right and wrong which are not
merely internalized by anyone, but describe the state of affairs
in which the same views are inculcated into the personality of
most members of a society, with most members of that society
stigmatizing deviations from them.

The sacred family was of course at all times partly a 'myth'. In
all societies there are always widespread infractions of the social
rules. In all societies, even the most pious, people succumb to
temptation against the dictates of their conscience. That does not
mean that therefore conduct in our non-pious and increasingly
non-family society is no different from conduct in any other, and
that any given form of behaviour is found with equal frequency
everywhere and at all times. For societies that orient the lives of
their members by the use of powerful myths are quite different
from those which have disposed of them. Some priests and even
some bishops fail to abide by their self-chosen vows of celibacy.
But it is the height of absurdity to imply from that, that the
average priest is indistinguishable from, say, the average student, or the average member of the media intelligentsia, in the
matter of self-control of sexuality in the interests of other people.
The rule of priestly celibacy itself was historically very important
in preserving the family life which celibacy precisely shuns. For
if celibacy is daily and publicly thus held up as a possibility, a
married couple can remain faithful even if one of them through
physical changes in middle or old age loses sexual interest, and

the other does not. If priestly celibacy is not possible, neither is life-long marital fidelity.

Within this socially-defined and socially-controlled institution called the family there were both structural injustices and many abuses resulting from conduct forbidden by the system. Each type of social system tends to produce its own characteristic type of abuse. That does not in itself condemn the system. Was the pre-1960s family so incorrigibly inclined to produce abuse of a man's position to secure for himself sexual gratification from his wife and daughters, and to lead to physical male violence against women, that it had to be dismantled altogether? Or would the dismantling of the family result in even more battering of women by men; even more exploitation of immature girls by transitory men, even by 'half' and 'step' relations, seeking nothing but sexual gratification or conquest; and other consequences, such as a new generation in which a higher proportion was stamped with problematical self-centredness (e.g. criminals)? To reveal faults in an institution is only to show again that all institutions are imperfect. To show abuses is only to show that the most perfect institution ever devised has been abused. Setting impossible goals may function for some as an effective incentive to achieve what is possible by way of improvement. But falling short of an imagined perfection can never be the criterion of whether or not an institution should continue to exist. It is always a matter of comparing one set of institutions with another in terms of specified, concrete results obtained in practice.[5]

Child-rearing and life-long mutual aid were of greater importance in the pre-1960s family than sex. Social interest in the latter stemmed mainly from the fact that uncontrolled sexuality had effects on the prospects of securing two full-time carers for the baby and infant, and on the chances of securing one person upon whom one other person could look for dutiful, guilt-guaranteed, unpaid services in, for example, illness and old age. The sexual *mores* were thus closely related to child-care and adult mutual aid, and it is in the area of sexual *mores* that change has been most obvious and indisputable.[6]

After a period of long and slow transformation, the sacred family quite suddenly lost most of its credibility, and (in a process that is, of course, far from complete) its place was taken by rational exchange. The 1990 report on British social attitudes[7] showed that only a very small minority of men and women aged 18-34 (6 per cent of both) believed by then that premarital sex was always or mostly wrong. Fewer than half of the women in this age group said that homosexual sex was always or mostly wrong. Among the young intelligentsia the proportion with these attitudes may be higher. Both authority elements and traditional elements are here, then, weak. There are strong free market elements. In terms of belief about what is morally objectionable or practically unwise the approved pattern is one of individual entrepreneurs, each free to strike a bargain as producer of sexual gratification with any willing consumer.

This does not carry with it the implication in the slightest degree that the relationship will be a 'promiscuous' one. The market is not synonymous with undiscriminating selection, though in practice there is impulsive and compulsive buying, sometimes regretted, just as there is what may be termed 'Dribergism'[8] in sexual relationships. A coupling pair may, and generally will, require of one another long-term commitments for the delivery of the agreed goods and services as part of a much larger package: 'a stable relationship'.

This is quite characteristic of a market situation. In the early 1990s the great commercial banks of Europe and the United States tended to redefine their promiscuity of the 1980s in granting loans ('transaction banking') as bad business, and advertised their conversion to the virtues of mutual long-term fidelity ('relationship banking'). Any purchaser of an automobile wants a stable relationship with the manufacturer and dealer. He wants a guarantee covering more years than most cohabiting couples in a stable relationship are prepared to give one another. What makes a relationship a market relationship is the emphasis on the *self-interest* of each of the parties—however much they might be of service to one another for a given period. Of course, the market only works when they believe they will be of service to one another.

The secularization and rationalization of the family appears to have been the work of sections of the middle class. The formerly shocking and subversive notions of permissive sex; the removal of the compulsions of religion, the law and stigma from the bond of permanent marriage; and the increase in choice in the destiny of the fertilized ovum, were in rapid succession condoned, then accepted, and then embraced. In the 1960s *the middle-class intelligentsia* were especially active and at the forefront of freeing indulgence in sexual intercourse from the irrational restrictions of socially inculcated 'conscience' and rules of conduct regarded as being absolutely binding regardless of the wishes or welfare of the particular individual.[9]

There was a notable increase in anti-Catholic-family sentiment from the early 1970s. In print and on television, prominence began to be given to the views of the new generation of feminists, in revolt against 'capitalist patriarchy' or 'patriarchal capitalism', whether as 'feminist Marxists', 'materialist feminists', or 'radical feminists'.[10] Television and the press, whatever their political bias, are biased in favour of the entertainment provided by the sensational. They are therefore more hospitable to the breaker than to the upholder of taboos. (They treated with sympathy demands that, for example, the veil of disgrace that the Catholic family drew over lesbian and male-homosexual sexual intercourse should be removed.)

Once the number and proportion of households which the male has never joined, or from which the male has absconded or been excluded, becomes large enough they constitute in themselves a formidable lobby. The lobby then opposes any cultural tendency to downgrade unfathered households. They must not be compared unfavourably in any way ('stigmatized') with families with fathers. Who may be partners with whom for sexual intercourse? Who shall supply the funds and personnel for child-care? Who will still love you when you're sixty-four? The household of the unmarried mother and the lone mother, the argument runs, is in principle as effective and desirable a way of solving these problems as is the family with a permanent father. Irrational stigma and the shortfall of reasonably and rightly available State benefits and State personnel and facilities account for any of the 'problems' of the fatherless household.

It has to be borne in mind, nevertheless, that the mass media's need to entertain is for all practical purposes insatiable, and any particular sacred cow must in the nature of things be sooner or later stripped of its sacredness and have to be discarded as an object for profanity. In due course, therefore, the quasi-sacred status successfully secured for the lone mother by her pressure-group advocates will render her in turn vulnerable to newcomers who are willing to express crudely and confidently the 'new', 'shocking', in media parlance 'sexy' idea that the spread of absent fatherhood is the social equivalent to the hole in the ozone layer and, for the average fatherless child, far more immediate and obvious in its consequences.

The numbers of young men and women brought together in universities and other centres of higher education increased rapidly in the 1960s. In Europe in particular, following the student unrest that culminated in the events of 1968, the 1970s saw a resurgence of interest in anarchist ideals. ('No name of magistrate;... riches, poverty, and use of service, none; contract, succession ... none; .. no sovereignty ... but nature should bring forth, of its own kind, all foison, all abundance, to feed my innocent people.'[11] True human nature is so constituted that when we are freed from all forms of authority, whether sacred or legal, the result will be creative, altruistic and peaceable co-operation.) It was virtually only on the Catholic family that anarchist ideas had (and still have) any effect, even though the 'families' of some of the eventually most notorious exponents of the idea, such as Charles Manson, came to such a bad end.[12]

The form of Marxism most popular with the student leaders, and generally providing the student activists with their ideology, was that of Herbert Marcuse. Marcuse and his fellow theorists of the so-called Frankfurt School saw revolution as no longer coming from the working class. The proletariat had been 'pacified' by capitalism, and was shackled by its own effort to be respectable. Revolution could now only come from those who were capable of rejecting the institutions of modern society: the pantheon of students, gays, the sexually liberated. In their 'Great Refusal' to conform to the norms of society 'the most advanced consciousness of humanity' (Marcuse and his school) meets with 'its most exploited force' (the heterogenous underclass). 'The people, previously the ferment of social change, have moved up to become the ferment of social cohesion. ... However, underneath the conservative popular base is the substratum of outcasts and outsiders, the exploited and persecuted of other races and other colours, the unemployed and the unemployable. Their opposition ... is an elementary force which violates the rules of the game and, in doing so, reveals it as a rigged game.'[13]

Trotskyism also had its few years of publicity—ending in England with the defeat in 1985 of the miners' year-long strike. Trotsky emphasized the importance of a 'Transitional Programme' as the prelude to the communist revolution, in effect, anything that destabilized society.[14] Trotskyists therefore looked benignly upon the disruption of the Catholic family, whether or not they believed that in the meantime its decline was damaging to this generation of adults and children: you cannot make omelettes without breaking eggs.

Members of this student generation—more or less well-informed about these ideas, and more or less conscious of them—came to prominence in the normal course of their careers in the media of mass communication in the 1970s and 1980s. Following the fashion, feminists of this generation plundered the works of Marx and Engels for analogies, metaphors, occasional direct references, and one favourite book, *The Origin of the Family, Private Property and the State*,[15] and then presented them as Marxist 'theories' of gender relations and child rearing. With its eclipse world-wide as a theory of the economy (whether temporarily, who knows?), it is only in its attack on the family that Marxism, with anarchism, retains a precarious refuge.

Among those who dropped their Marxism altogether, what the Soviet Union had once been as a model of the desirable future in family matters, Sweden now became, as it was already for many non-Marxist socialists and liberals.

The increased pace of the liberation of individuals from the family as an institution, freeing them to follow their own rationally-calculated self-interest, cannot be plausibly attributed in the light of Marxist doctrine to economic forces operating on the English proletariat (the collapse of community life following the demise of the old heavy industries, the disappearance of the disciplines afforded by apprenticeships, poor job prospects, unemployment and low wages). In so far as economic forces did operate according to Marxist tenets, they did so by providing the material riches which were, for Marx, the condition of choice freed from economic determination. Economic forces created, that is, the broad class of the well-to-do in prosperous capitalist societies. The new sexual and child-care morality was not the creation of the proletariat under the *stress* of economic necessity, but of that part of the bourgeoisie furthest *removed* from economic necessity, in the media of communication and especially of entertainment.

Middle class men were soon absenting themselves from inconvenient parenting duties as frequently as men of the lower working class. Men were quite suddenly denuded of the internalized sense of a quasi-sacred duty to their sexual partner, to their children's mother, and to their children. The onerous tasks connected with being the 'father' to a child, to an infant and eventually to a youth possibly as obstreperous as he knows himself to be, became avoidable. In these circumstances it was quite natural that fatherhood was increasingly evaded. Even though into the 1990s the majority of men still became and remained for their lifetime good fathers from out-dated motives and on a host of other grounds, the trend was strongly against them. The sense among their kinsfolk, their neighbours, the people they worked with and for was similarly attenuated. In particular the cultural messages they received in their entertainment and instruction were almost purely messages that equated one mode of dealing with sex and parenthood with any other mode. In this social atmosphere ever-larger numbers of biological fathers—invited to be undertakers of nothing but the easy, pleasant and exciting task of sexual intercourse itself—rationally eschewed the heavy risks and responsibilities of sociological parenthood.

As the Marxist-feminist attack on the family is the last fling of Marxism, the Catholic family was the last bastion against what in England (and indeed throughout the world) was in the 1980s popularly thought of as Thatcherism—leaving social organization to the forces of the market—and the progressive middle class brought down its walls.

The same applied to the reforming intelligentsia's treatment of the onerous and difficult tasks and adjustments necessary to live in reasonable harmony with someone else for years on end in the intimacy of a household. With all imaginable assistance from sound experience and lessons carried into adulthood from the parental home, from secular and religious instruction, from benign neighbourhood *mores*, this remains a daunting prospect for the most mature and wise human being. The media middle class vigorously set about dismantling the culture that had allowed the same small group of people to live together under one roof for very long periods.

Much of the 'housing shortage' and 'homelessness' in modern societies is due to the fact that the given population is simply splitting into smaller and smaller units of people able or willing to live together. The number of single-person households, people making a home with not even one other person, once mainly created by the death of a partner, was rapidly added to by people who did not want anyone to interfere with their domestic privacy and freedom to eat and play as they pleased.[16]

In societies in which there are strong pressures to keep him fixated on his personal interests, if the family bargain looks unfavourable to him the biological father does not enter it: if the bargain he has struck becomes a bad one, the rational person withdraws from it as soon as he can. As they say in the literature, he 'exits'.

There was thus, by the 1990s, very largely a market situation in the production and distribution of the goods and services which *earlier in the century* had been restricted to or were the special business of the strictly controlled two-parent family. In 1992 Gallup Poll questioned a sample of women with children aged from newborn to 18. Among those mothers aged between 16 and 24, half were single. Culturally what was even more significant was that almost 50 per cent of the total sample, not just the single mothers, *approved* of a woman choosing to have a child outside of *any* 'stable relationship with a man' (not merely outside of marriage).[17] Well-documented and unchallengeable statistics in the carefully controlled area of the recording of births and deaths in a country like England show a marked decline in the illegitimacy rate in the first half of the twentieth century; the two decades following 1970 showed a very rapid and large increase. The relevance of the argument sometimes heard that illegitimacy was higher than it is today at some time in the more or less remote past—the sixteenth century, say—is therefore difficult to grasp.

On the other measure of unreliability for the child in its supply of 'fathering', there is no evidence yet that the growing proportion of unmarried couples who jointly register their child have a relationship on the average as stable as those married even under present conditions. In the meanwhile, it is prima facie at least as unlikely, rather than prima facie likely that such relationships will prove as stable when they come to be investigated.

Are the effects of never-present or otherwise absent fathers important? Here we want to recall the distinction made above between the biological and the sociological father, between 'the father' and 'fathering'. Just as Dr John Bowlby in a now much abused and much unread book emphasizes 'mothering', and insists that the best 'mothering' need not be supplied by the mother, or even by a female, (it can be 'a permanent mother-substitute'),[18] so *in principle* 'fathering' can be supplied by anyone. It is simply still factually more likely to be supplied in our society, if at all, by a man, that man being the biological father.

The initiation of social policy, to say nothing of its ultimate success, depends upon the alignment of political forces. One of the two consenting parties to sexual intercourse will always *physically* get off scot free, while the other may become pregnant. Strict arrangements were in force in the pre-1960s system to redress the balance by means of the socialization and social control of the man. The normal inclination of a socialist is to be alert to the unforeseen and unintended consequences of bargains for one or other of the bargainers. Thus he will be the first to point out (to take a homely example) that a piece of cling film, produced and purchased in good faith, after all contaminates the pork chop that it covers. The remote chance of damage to the willing purchaser makes the production of cling film a matter which requires some degree of abatement of rational exchange by the intervention of the public authorities. In his market-orientation to family matters, this same socialist is strangely obtuse to the asymmetrical consequences for the bargainers for pleasurable sexual intercourse 'if things go wrong'.

He is also normally sensitive to third-party effects. Motor cars pollute the atmosphere with their exhaust fumes; individual motorists might not mind; the manufacturers might not mind, so cars are willingly bought and sold. But not only the motorist, the motorless pedestrian also suffers from the poisonous gases. Market freedom must be modified in the public interest by rational law.

On the other hand, 'Thatcherites' (if we may once more be permitted that shorthand term, even though she no longer stands at the dispatch box) are slower to accept that rational-legal action—the State—is the best instrument for curing the ills of rational individual or group exchange, and are also less ready to recognize the possibilities of unforeseen damage to the one or both parties to a contract.

But in the matter of the whole range of the precious goods and services involved in parenthood and marriage we have a curious reversal of roles.

The reversal is easy to understand on the modern, *laissez-faire*, political right. Adam Smith always emphasized the importance of some—a very considerable—part in society for rational law. Many classical-liberal thinkers, not least the most prominent among them, Hayek, have fully recognized the importance of certain absolutely-believed-in—what we have called quasi-religious—values if any social system, including the 'free market', is to work.

What is difficult to understand, but it is a highly salient fact, is the refusal of American liberals and European socialists to examine the fresh and strong free market elements that have now invaded the area of sex and sociological 'fatherhood'. Subject only to his finding another equally free party to strike the sexual bargain in the first place, sociological fatherhood has become a relationship which a man is substantially free to enter or not as he pleases, even if he does beget children; and it has become a relationship that he can leave with now almost complete freedom if the bargain no longer suits him, with the legal (as distinct from the emotional) consequences for him being limited at worst to monetary payments.

Liberals and socialists in this area quite uncharacteristically deny or minimize the importance of third-party effects. It is they, not the radical right, who insist that for the child there is nothing to choose between the many household arrangements created by the system of rational voluntary exchange—no differences 'as such'. In so far as there is more harm to the child in one than another, the solution is exclusively hard cash, invariably dismissed in other contexts as a capitalist cure-all. 'The family is not deteriorating it is just changing.'

That liberals and socialists should extol the virtues of the cash nexus at the expense of relationships based on mutual service and long-term trust is perhaps the most unexpected phenomenon of all.

Yet if the findings of the studies we have examined are representative of all studies, from a socialist point of view the most serious 'externality' ought to be on the agenda, and distinctly is not. The studies show, and sociological and psychological theory explain, that unless a child is brought up in the constant atmosphere of human beings negotiating the business of getting on with one another, co-operating, controlling their anger, affecting reconciliations, he cannot learn what it is to be an effective member of a social group. He can only learn this as he learns his native tongue, by experiencing the phenomenon, in this case social interaction, taking place outside of himself, yet his being part of it *densely and continuously*. For this he needs the presence of two adults in close interaction constantly in his immediate environment. (He needs a great many other relationships besides, of course. A child, whatever his family background, will tend to benefit from, say, a suitable creche experience.[19] He learns not only social interaction as such, but also as he grows older particular forms of social interaction, such as what it looks like and what it means to undertake disciplined, time-bound tasks outside the household, as well as in the household tasks. He learns cognitively and internalizes cathetically, through social interaction, the expressive features of roles and the instrumental features of roles.)

The literature sometimes contains assertions that the absence of the father is not a serious problem because the slack can be and is taken up by members of the extended family. But extended families themselves exist only because of the practice of long-term marriage. The marriage bond not only creates the 'husband' and 'wife'. It also creates 'uncles' and 'aunts' and 'grandmothers' and 'grandfathers' with a long-term relationship to the child. Churches created a backstop—the 'god mother' and the 'god father'. Although these were probably never very effective, they were at least created out of the insight that long-term responsibility, on the basis of something additional to self-interest, was of value to the child. When marriage is weakened, the whole network of kin is weakened, and the present generation of one-parent families, where they are fortunate enough to be able to depend on kinsfolk, are depending upon a wasting asset.

On the overwhelming evidence, the child who to a greater or lesser degree lacks a sociological father grows up more independent of his fellows and less able or willing to undertake social duties. We have therefore a dilemma or contradiction appearing. The absence of the father means for a large majority of their children dependence on material resources being provided through the State. In a multi-party democracy this essentially means fellow-citizens demonstrating willingness through the ballot box to undertake a social duty to care for their fellows and for future generations. But already the classic phrases of rampant capitalism come to mind as the numbers of fatherless families mount, 'Cannot a man do what he likes with his own? As for the other party, *caveat emptor*—let her take the consequences of her own bad bargain!'

There is nobility in individualism, when the reasonably foreseeable consequences are taken by the actor himself. For most liberals and socialists it is—or at the very least once was—the aim of State control and State assistance to foster it. It is an entirely different matter when in sexual conduct the cast of mind is that I please myself, but if anything goes wrong, you must be responsible that my children come to no harm. In effect such a biological father is saying, 'You must be a socialist so that I can be an egoist. My baby is the hostage through whom I, who will not do my duty, will hold you to your duty.' It is the ultimate corruption of both individualistic and socialistic ideals. But it is the greater betrayal of the latter: it is egoistic socialism.

Cultural capital can go to waste no less than physical capital; only, when it happens it is more difficult to see. Families without fathers produce egoists. We become a society of fatherless families, of men temporarily attached to households of a woman and her children, and not an integral and permanent part of them. When the process is far enough spent, by what magic, then, will we be able to produce the dutiful citizens who will protect their partners and their children from their economic and cultural disadvantages?

Notes

1 Absence from the *acceptance of responsibility* for the welfare and rearing of his children is the key concept, rather than physical absence as such, which may be part-and-parcel of a high and effective exercise of such responsibility.

2 Bede, *A History of the English Church and People* (731 A.D.), Harmondsworth: Penguin, 1968, pp. 74-83.

3 *Familiaris Consortio: Apostolic Exhortation of His Holiness Pope John Paul II to the Episcopate, to the Clergy and to the Faithful of the Whole Catholic Church Regarding the Role of the Christian Family in the Modern World*, London: Catholic Truth Society, 1981.

4 *Op. cit.*, pp. 163-64.

5 Dennis, N., and Halsey, A.H., *English Ethical Socialism: St. Thomas More to R.H. Tawney*, Oxford: Clarendon Press, 1988, *passim*.

6 There was fornication, adultery and (as everyone knows) homosexual sex in London in the 1890s. In our society the sufferer from the most serious of the venereal diseases is accorded the status of one of Schiller's 'sublime criminals', and is more often portrayed simply as a martyr to the cause of sexual freedom. But when Ibsen's realistic, conventionally moralistic and harshly condemnatory treatment of a parent wrecking his child's health through syphilis, *Ghosts*, was played at the Royalty Theatre, London, in

1891, there was a cry of outrage from the secular organs of sober opinion. 'This disgusting representation ... injecting the modern theatre with poison ... an open drain ... a loathsome sore unbandaged ... a dirty act done publicly ... candid foulness ... putrid indecorum ... literary carrion ... crapulous ... perilous nuisance.' (From an anthology of press reactions to the first London performance of *Ghosts*, compiled by William Archer, 'Ghosts and Gibberings', *Pall Mall Gazette*, 8 April 1891. See also H.A. Kennedy, 'The Drama of the Moment', *Nineteenth Century*, 30, 1891, pp. 258-74.) It may be possible to argue from one's own moral code that sexual liberation has made ours a better society; but it is impossible to argue from the facts that all that has happened is, that what now occurs without concealment occurred previously to much the same extent in secret.

7   *British Social Attitudes: Seventh Report*, London: Gower Publications, 1990.

8   Tom Driberg, a considerable figure in English public life in his time, as an M.P., a peer of the realm, and a popular journalist, eventually revealed in his autobiography that he had been, and was unashamedly unremitting in his search for homosexual sexual intercourse. Tom Driberg [Baron Bradwell], *Ruling Passions*, London: Jonathan Cape, 1977.

9   See Hotchner, A.E., *Blown Away: the Rolling Stones and the Death of the Sixties*, New York: Simon and Schuster, 1990. The message of popular rock groups can be summed up in the manifesto of Jim Morrison, lead singer of The Doors (roughly America's Rolling Stones): 'Erotic politicians, that's what we are. We're interested in everything about revolt, disorder, and all activity that appears to have no meaning'.

10 Kramarae, C., and Treichler, P.A., *A Feminist Dictionary*, London: Unwin Hyman Pandora, 1985.

11 *The Tempest*, II, i. Shakespeare puts in Gonzalo's mouth a version of Montaigne's ideal society.

12 Saunders, E., *The Family: The Story of Charles Manson's Dune Buggy Attack Battalion*, London: Rupert Hart-Davis, 1971.

13 Marcuse, H., *One Dimensional Man: Studies in the Ideology of Advanced Industrial Society*, Boston: Beacon Press, 1964, pp. 256-57.

14 Trotsky, L., *Transitional Programme: The Death Agony of Capitalism and the Tasks of the Fourth International* (1938), London: The Other Press, 1979.

15 (1884). Harmondsworth: Penguin, 1985. Introduction by Barrett, M., member of the editorial collective of *Feminist Review*, author of *Women's Oppression Today: Problems in Marxist Feminist Analysis* (1980), and joint author of *The Anti-social Family* (1982).

16   In 1973 9 per cent of the population of Great Britain 16 years of age or older lived alone. This had increased to 13 per cent by 1989. Among the older generation there was hardly any change in the proportion living alone—the figure went up from 26 per cent to 27 per cent. But among the 16-24-year-olds the figure went up from 2 per cent to 4 per cent, and among the 25-44-year-olds it trebled from 2 per cent to 6 per cent. *General Household Survey 20, 1989*, London: HMSO, 1991.

17   *The Times* (15 July 1992) dealt with the survey under the headline, 'Women count the cost of parenthood'. Attention was focused, that is, on the burdens of motherhood. Three-quarters of the mothers felt that the most important thing they had lost was 'time to devote to their own personal care and exercise'. Even as recently as eighteen years before, when these women began to have their babies, almost certainly the findings on the disappearance of the man from the household of the child, and especially women's approval of it, would have predominated in public comment.

18   Bowlby, J., *Child Care and the Growth of Love*, Harmondsworth: Penguin, 1953, p. 12.

19   Paper presented by Dr. Bengt-Erik Andersson, Fourth European Conference on Developmental Psychology, University of Stirling, Scotland, 28 August 1990.

7

The Consequences for
Fellow Citizens

'Teenage glue sniffers are believed to be responsible for the damage
caused to thousands of books during an orgy of destruction after two
break-ins. Books were piled knee-deep on the floor of the building
after all the shelves were overturned and the cleaning fluids and
other liquids stored in the library were poured over the volumes.'[1]

'A Wearside woman ... has been burgled 26 times ... Since the raids
started six years ago, thousands of pounds worth of property has
vanished from her council flat.'[2]

The vast majority of the innumerable transactions of ordinary
daily life in the United Kingdom are peaceable. They are co-
operative. Or they do not involve interference with the welfare of
others. Or interference is tolerated as part of the give and take
of social existence.

At the level of any single 'corrupt politician', any 'burglar', any
industrialist breaking the safety laws, any 'crooked businessman', any 'foul-mouthed lout', on the average he or she differs
from his honest or decently-behaved counterpart only in that the
one is a villain in, say, 10 per cent of his activities, while the
other in, say, one per cent. Even the 10 per cent of bad behaviour
is substantially reduced for those who are willing to accept his
terms of interaction and his self-image as heroic contender
against, or the helpless victim of an already incorrigibly vicious
world. 'When a felon's not engaged in his employment', as Gilbert
and Sullivan rightly point out, 'or concocting his felonious little
plans, his capacity for innocent enjoyment is just as great as any
other man's'.

On the other hand, it is a matter of very little interest, because
it is both endemic and obvious, that 'there has always been' this
or that form of social misconduct and self-abuse; and of course
there have been some periods in the history of this country, and

some particular places, and some special sections of the population when or where things have been much worse than they are today.

The important question is, in the here and now are things getting better or worse; are they getting better or worse rapidly or slowly; if worse, is the change reversible; and if reversible, by what means?

All societies prohibit in principle the acquisition of the control over goods and other people except in accordance with the existing rules governing property and violence. The core of the meaning of violations of those rules of control over property and over invasions of the integrity of the person through assault or insult —'theft', 'rape', and so on—remains stable and understandable across cultures whatever the detailed differences in definition.

The sort of transactions listed in a criminal code do not by any means constitute the full catalogue of the misdeeds a person can inflict on others or on herself. Many of the transactions listed in a society's criminal code take place and remain unrecorded, from the equivalent to cases of shoplifting to business fraud on a large scale.

Nevertheless, if the trend in recorded crime were inexorably upward, it cannot be supposed there would be significant movements towards less self-centred and away from socially and personally disruptive conduct in other spheres of social life, or that the reported figures would systematically be moving in one direction and the 'dark figures' in the opposite direction. Unless there were convincing evidence to the contrary, therefore, the trend in crime can be taken as an index of the trend in self- and other-regarding behaviour in a society.

In the recent past a group of customary exhortations, legal requirements, and legal prohibitions held together in a single bundle, much more tightly than today, the four activities of sex, procreation, child rearing, and non-commercial, personal and permanent adult mutual-aid. Both as an explicit function and through the experiences the child had within such a structure, one of the principal effects of this tightly-bound system was to heavily inculcate into the child the skills, and more importantly the motivations, necessary for law-abidingness. In the late 1960s and the 1970s the student Marxists, Critical Sociologists, radical psychiatrists, feminists and New Criminologists discovered to their horror that the family was about 'socialization and social control', about the 'production and reproduction of social labour'. Anyone outside their circles could only wonder that they had taken so long to stumble upon this very open secret. They needed to have looked no further than Cranmer's influential formulation, familiar for centuries to everyone married according to the rites of the Church of England.[3]

In assessing the significance of the recent disintegration of the *mores*[4] of the nuclear family (as that term was understood until the mid-1960s), therefore, what has been happening to the range of behaviours classified as crime must be considered. The frequency of crime is not only intrinsically important to those who suffer from its direct consequences and from its indirect consequences in the quality of everyone's life when it loses the element of trusting one's fellows. It is also (with all its defects) the best available index of the growth and decline of anti-social conduct, of the growth and decline of 'civility', in general.

In an official Home Office study of crime in the 1980s, Mayhew, Elliott and Dowds give the impression that a significant explanation of the increase in the crime figures is simply the increase in the public's reporting of it. The 1988 British Crime Survey (BCS), they write, 'Shows that overall crime as measured by the BCS [the BCS was a study of the victims of both reported and unreported crime] has risen significantly less since 1981 than offences reported to the police. This suggests that both the reporting and recording of crimes is increasing, giving the impression that crime is rising faster than it is in fact.'

There are five objections to the authors' statement, which as it stands can be taken to support the assertions of the 'folk devils and moral panic' school of criminology, that the 'rise in crime' is an illusion, and the figures that appear in the statistics are merely an artifact of increased reporting of an unchanged volume of crimes.

The first is that the everyday meaning of the word 'significance' can be confused with its technical meaning in statistics. A divergence that is small and socially unimportant ('socially insignificant') may nevertheless be statistically significant, that is, unlikely to be attributable to chance. The 1988 BCS actually says that, taking 1981-87 as a whole, 'generally there has been a flatter rise in BCS estimates than in recorded offences ... the divergence is statistically significant'.

In fact both crime reported to the police and crime disclosed by the BCS both rose rapidly 1981-87, and the divergence between the two sets of figures is statistically, but not socially, significant.

The second is that the figures are quite mixed. The rate at which vandalism was reported to the police between 1981 and 1987 did increase much more rapidly than the rate at which the BCS shows vandalism was experienced as taking place—the police figures 'over-reported' vandalism's increase in the period. But under-reporting of burglary without loss (still not a pleasant event in one's life) increased considerably, and under-reporting even of burglary with loss, where insurance is involved, increased to some extent. Only two of the crimes listed show a divergence between crimes reported to the police and crimes reported in the victim survey which is statistically significant at the 5 per cent level, vandalism and bicycle theft.

The divergence in the case of vandalism shows over-reporting. (There was still on the victims' figures a 10 per cent increase.) But in the case of bicycle theft, on the contrary, the statistically significant divergence was one showing an increase in *under-reporting*. The large percentage rise in bicycle thefts experienced by the victims in the BCS survey (up 80 per cent) contrasts with the percentage change in bicycle thefts reported to the police (up 5 per cent). (Some might sneer at the triviality of bicycle theft. But for the child whose bicycle is stolen, or who expects it to be stolen if it is unsupervised for a few moments, it is a fact which becomes part and parcel of her quality of life, of her perception of other people as trustworthy or not.)

The third is that the BCS, the victims' survey, makes it clear that in most of the years, and notably in the later years of the period, 1983-87, while the divergence was 'too small to reach statistical significance', officially recorded crime had risen by 26 per cent and the crime disclosed in the BCS had risen by nearly as much, by 21 per cent—a matter of considerable social significance.

The fourth is that more people thought it was pointless to report the crime to the police. Of all crimes not reported because of the belief that the police would not do anything about them there was a rise from 16 per cent in 1984 to 21 per cent in 1988. Of those not reporting vandalism, 18 per cent in 1984 did not report it because they thought the police would do nothing. This had risen to 26 per cent by 1988. The equivalent figures for theft from motor vehicle showed a rise from 21 per cent in 1984 to 30 per cent in 1988. Burglary with loss showed a rise from 12 per cent to 21 per cent. Assault showed a rise from 6 per cent to 9 per cent. Robbery showed a rise from 21 per cent to 30 per cent.

The fifth is that the 'lower' percentage rises of the crime victims' survey refer to historically very large numbers of incidents. 'There were an estimated 13 million incidents in 1987 falling into the BCS categories of crimes against individuals and their private property.'[5] Victims experienced nearly three million cases of vandalism in the year, of which only one in ten were reported to the police (305,000), and over two million cases of theft from a motor vehicle, of which somewhat over a quarter were reported to the police (626,000).

The British Crime Survey's estimates of the actual percentage rise in offences in England and Wales in the period 1981-87 were: bicycle theft, up 80 per cent; burglary attempts without loss, up 78 per cent; theft from a motor vehicle, up 63 per cent; and theft of a motor vehicle up 36 per cent. In 1987 22 per cent of all owners of vehicles were the target of some sort of vehicle crime, and 2.5 per cent had their car driven away without their consent. Burglary with loss was up 39 per cent. None of the increases corresponds to the percentage rises in the period in the quantity or value of goods available to be stolen.[6]

After examining the records of the first generation of boys experiencing the new morality of the 1960s, those aged 14 in 1967, a Home Office study showed that by the time they were 31, in 1984, one in three males had been convicted of a standard-list offence.[7] This figure must be seen against the background, sketched above, of the large number and proportion of crimes not reported by the victim to the police, and of the large number of offences known to the police that do not end in a conviction. It must also be seen against the background of the 'dark figure' of immoral legal behaviour and crime in business and commerce. The rich and the powerful, however so tainted and corrupt, are much more likely than the poor and impotent to keep their typical misdeeds outside of the criminal codes, their own violations of the criminal code obscure and, when exposed, be able to manipulate the system so as to escape a guilty verdict.

It was no consolation to council-estate victims of council-estate criminals to be assured by post-1970s social-policy academics that there was more and worse white-collar crime, and by New Criminologists and Trotskyists that the criminals were, as we have already remarked, 'prefigurative revolutionaries'.

Gallup International's survey carried out in November 1984 showed that a home in Britain was more than twice as likely to have been broken into than a home in West Germany, and four times more likely than a home in Belgium (16 per cent, 7 per cent, 4 per cent respectively). In 1984 there were 653 thefts of cars per 100,000 population in Britain, as contrasted with 118 per 100,000 population in West Germany.

In 1983 a representative British sample was asked, 'Here is a list of predictions about problems Britain might face. For each one, please say how likely or unlikely you think it is to come true in Britain within the next ten years.' Fifty per cent believed that the police would find it impossible to protect our personal safety on the streets. Only 8 per cent thought that it was not at all likely. 56 per cent replied that it was very likely or quite likely that riots and civil disturbances would become common. Only 5 per cent said it was not at all likely.[8] In 1984 37 per cent of British people polled said they were afraid to answer their door at night. Eight years later the figure was 54 per cent.[9]

The increase in crime is a feature of all large urban populations. In non-authoritarian societies—'free' in the sense that social order depends upon self-control rather than control by agents of the State—crimes increase to the extent that the mechanisms of socialization and the *mores* lose their ability to reproduce and maintain a culture of decent mutual respect, trust, and restraint.

The North-Western University Center for Urban Affairs and Policy Research, Chicago, studied crime trends in the 396 cities in the United States with a population of more than 50,000. Even in the such thriving cities as San Jose and Phoenix, at the bottom end of the scale of the increase in crime, property crimes doubled and violent crimes quadrupled between 1948 and 1978. The highest growth in the crime rate was found in the declining city of Newark, New Jersey, where there was a sevenfold rise in property crime, and an elevenfold increase in violent crime. 'Whether local officials engaged in Herculean efforts or none at all, the crime wave affected their community.' The authors attribute the rise partly to the greater attractiveness of crime when affluence makes more goods of higher value available to the criminal, but partly also to the growth of the pool of potential offenders.[10]

In authoritarian and totalitarian societies crime extends beyond the corruption of the elites when they lose or give up their power to hold their populations in check with unremitting propaganda, close supervision and condign punishment. Yeltsin's St. Petersburg was much more crime-ridden than Stalin's Leningrad, and Kohl's east Berlin than either Hitler's or Honecker's.

But the power of self-control necessary for a free society is clearly shown by the figures for this country in the midst of its urban-industrial growth, and the weakening of the power of self-control by the trend of the figures in the past thirty years.

In 1861, when the population of England and Wales was 20 million, 88,000 indictable offences were recorded by the police. In the year 1990, when the population was 50 million, 4.3 million notifiable offences (excluding criminal damage of £20 or under) were recorded by the police.

The population was two-and-a-half times as large. The crime figure was 50 times as large.

In 1861 the rate was under 500 per 100,000 of the population.

In 1990 it was over 8,600 per 100,000 of the population.[11] (Figure, p. 124.)

When every known and correctable defect of the figures has been attended to; when every reasonable estimate has been made for defects the magnitude of which can only be intelligently gauged; and when the benefit of every doubt is given to those whose elitist speculations are directed at showing that the ignorant and misguided population at large suffers under an illusion that crime has increased, what is left is a massive increase in criminal activity in British society.

This is especially true of the rise in the crime rates during the past thirty years. Difficulties multiply in comparing figures from 1861 with those of 1991, because of everything from changes in classification (though burglary fundamentally remains burglary, and assault, assault), new categories of crime such as taking a vehicle without consent (though there were equivalents such as horses and bicycles in previous periods), changes in police numbers and practices, to changes in means of reporting crime (though it was not much more difficult at one time to contact the foot patrolman on the beat than, until quite recently, contact the station from a phone box).

But these changes do not have an impact from year to year, and those which do (such as a change in the value of damage for it to count as 'criminal', notifiable, damage) can be taken account of in any analysis.

The crime figure in 1955 was recognizably of the same magnitude as that of 1861. There were five times that year's number of offences in 1955, in a population more than twice as large. In a century the crime rate per 100,000 had about doubled, from 438 to 1,040.

In contrast, from 1955 to 1989 the number of crimes increased eight-fold, and the crime rate increased seven-fold. The *increase* in the *single year* 1990-91, 733,000,[12] was eight or more times the *total* annual figure, year by year and decade by decade at the end of the nineteenth and the beginning of the twentieth century.[13]

The national annual crime rate averaged 271 per 100,000 at its low point in the period before the Great War (1910-14). In the Northumbria police area (mainly the Tyneside towns and Sunderland) the rate in 1989 was 12,684. If the communities of

Tyneside and Wearside had been roughly as civil as the rest of the country in the earlier period (and there are many reasons for believing that they were, if not more so), in the life-time of a 77-year-old the average citizen has become 47 times more likely to be the victim of a crime against his or her person or property.

The *rise* in crime in England and Wales between 1985 and 1990 was roughly equivalent to the *total* annual crime as late as 1938.[14]

In 1991 there were almost as many cases of the *single* crime of violence against the person (190,000) as there had been total crimes (195,000 annual average) during each of the years 1930-34, the great unemployment period of the Thirties. Within a period of only eight years the increase in this single offence of violence against the person was over one-third of the figure for all crimes in an average year in the 1930s.[15]

'Wounding and other acts endangering life' is a crime not likely to be greatly affected within a period of a few years by changes in definition or other factors which create a gap between reality and statistical records. It steadily and rapidly doubled in the decade of the 1980s, from 4,400 in 1980 to 8,900 in 1990. Another offence which is characterized by its relative lack of ambiguity and by the likelihood that occurrences will be recorded is that 'where firearms are reported to have been used'. The first volume of *Criminal Statistics* in which figures appear for this offence is that for 1976, where they are carried back to 1970. Again, there is a smooth and rapid acceleration, from 1,400 in 1970, to seven times that number, 10,400, twenty years later. The increase in the one year 1989-90 (870) was more than half the total of 1970.[16]

The issue of the 1908 volume of *Criminal Statistics* was taken as an occasion for a review of the trends in crime over the previous fifty years, the first volume of the predecessor of *Criminal Statistics* having appeared in 1857. Rather than the figure of crimes known to the police or other possible series of statistics available from 1857, the author takes the total of 'persons for trial or tried for indictable offences' as the best index, not of the volume of crime at any one time—there is always a more or less indefinite 'dark figure' of unreported and undetected crime—but of fluctuations in crime. Whichever series was considered, however, each showed over the fifty years the same 'steady decline' in crime, with only 'occasional slight interruptions'.

In 1857 the total figure was 54,667.

This had increased to 59,079 by 1906.

Proportionately to population, crime had diminished by about 40 per cent.

The author, not being of course familiar with the entirely different scale of modern annual increases, not to speak of increases over the past half-a-century, speaks of 'considerable' variations over the period, though the difference between the highest and lowest figures in the fifty-year period was only 15,000, the total never exceeding 63,000 (in 1882) nor falling below 48,000 (in 1860).

Over a period in which the population grew from 19 million to 34 million, the *total* number of 'offences against the person' in the whole country rose by only 228, from only 2,258 in 1857 to 2,546 in 1906. (As compared with this rise of 228 in fifty years, in 1991 alone crimes against the person rose by over 90,000, from 100,200 to 190,300.)

Well could Conan Doyle introduce the Sherlock Holmes series in 1887 with the celebrated detective suffering from ennui in a city which was purgatory for the devoted criminologist (as he described himself), lacking as it did the crimes necessary to give interest to his life.[17] Well could Dean Inge in 1917 write that the Great War had awoken a sense of fear for the integrity of the home and the safety of women and children, 'a feeling to which modern civilized man *had long been a stranger'*.[18]

In the face of such a growth in overall population, 'offences of violence' had actually declined in absolute numbers, from 1,737 to 1,443. Sexual offences—these absolute figures relate to the whole of England and Wales—rose from 421 to 1,103. 'Prosecutions for riot, common fifty years ago, are now comparatively rare.' There were 157 such prosecutions in 1857, only 26 in 1906.

The more serious non-indictable offences, too, showed a 'considerable decline' over the fifty years. The less serious of the non-indictable offences (the non-indictable offences themselves being mainly less serious than indictable offences) had grown from 215,800 to 618,714. Less serious non-indictable offences had nearly trebled, that is, during a period in which the population had nearly doubled. The existence of the new School Boards from 1870 meant that 'education offences', from being none in 1857, were running at 57,399 in 1906. The progressive establishment of local police forces from the 1830s saw 'contravening police regulations' rising from 28,633 to 132,504.[19]

During 1938, when Sunderland's population was 186,000, there were about three reported cases a week of burglary and housebreaking, and about three larcenies a week from vehicles, shops, and meters. In the whole year there were eight cases of rape and five of wounding. There were no reported cases of murder, manslaughter, infanticide, unnatural offences and attempts, or malicious injury to property. In those days in a working class town like Sunderland pedal cycles were comparable in number and importance to the car today; it was unusual for cycles to be locked, and they were reported stolen at the rate of about one a week.[20]

A vignette of law and order in Sunderland at about this time: Three working-class boys, a 12-year-old with his pal and his pal's 14-year-old brother, having played truant from Sunday School, are sharing a Woodbine at the loading bay at the back of Blackett's, a town-centre department store. A policeman appears at one end of the back lane, another at the other. Smoking the cigarette is misbehaviour, and they are about to get into trouble for that alone, not because they are suspected of something worse. Probably the policemen smoke, probably the boys' fathers smoke. But the boys are not allowed to smoke at their age; and policemen and fathers believe it is better if the boys do not acquire the addiction, waste their money and damage their lungs at any age.

That is the way the policemen define the situation, and it is the way the boys define the situation. The eldest boy goes in one direction, the two youngest in the other. The pair then make a dart for it, one of them actually through the policeman's legs, and away they run. But the pursuing policeman swings and throws his gas-mask case, and the slower of the two is hit on the back of the head, falls to the ground and is captured. The swifter of the two runs the mile-and-a-half home, and sits outside the house waiting anxiously for the result. Sure enough, both the brothers have been caught, and the two policemen appear in the street. The policemen tell the father. The boy is given 'a good telling off' by his father, and is glad to escape 'a clip' or worse.

There is not the slightest thought on the any of the working-class parents' part that the policemen were doing anything but the right thing, and not the slightest thought on the part of either the policemen, or the parents, or the boys, that there could possibly be any journalist who would define the situation publicly as 'a disgraceful assault on a schoolchild', or as 'a victimless crime', or as 'a waste of police resources on a triviality, in war-time too!', or as something that 'the boy will inevitably do if his parents do it', or 'smoking is a feature of working-class culture'—or that there could be any editor who would print any of it if it were written.

Such social control was pervasive and consensual, and therefore low-key, good-humoured and effective.[21]

The story was told to one of the authors in mid-1992 by one of the culprits, a former shipyard welder (by then a successful husband, father and grandfather), not to criticize the harshness of the old working-class culture in Sunderland, but to deplore the consequences of the new media-driven non-culture.

Another contribution on the same subject came from a second humane and egalitarian husband, father and grandfather, whose whole working life had been spent as a Sunderland coal-miner. Shortly after he had been made redundant in the mid-1980s he had been in the nearby colliery town of Easington. The memorial to the 83 men who had been killed in the mine in 1951 had been defaced, and he had kept a note of the defacement in his wallet to this day. 'To honour the memory of those who lost their lives. Let passers-by do likewise, get understanding and promote goodwill in all things.' Over these words someone had scrawled, 'the Parky stinks of F*** Head'.

We feel that such witnesses of cultural and non-cultural events and changes should be taken at least as seriously as the definers of the situation who have come to dominate the principal, and especially the new media of communication in the course of the past twenty or thirty years.

We sometimes encounter academics whose own knowledge of working-class life, in time-span and amount of direct contact, is extremely limited, who brusquely dismiss such experience as worthless 'anecdote' and the statistics as a ruling-class fabrication. What is remarkable, however, is the facility with which some of the more confident and vocal have concluded, against such 'romanticizing anecdotes' and against such 'flawed statistics' that the anecdotes and the statistics give the wrong version of the 'underprivileged' present as compared with this century's working-class past. Even more remarkably, with no statistics and few if any direct reports ('anecdotes'?) to support anything they say, some claim to provide the correct version.

Leaving data to one side altogether, their position is quite unsustainable in logic. For even if they could demonstrate that the evidence for one particular version of reality were ill-based they would not be thereby demonstrating that the version was wrong. Much less does demonstrating that one particular version of reality is ill-based thereby prove that an alternative version, lacking any factual basis at all, is right. On their own argument, there is only one thing that these academics who attribute no value to crime statistics, and repudiate the commonplaces of the beliefs about their past lives of older working-class people, could ever show. That would be that, for total lack of evidence, nobody could now compare, and nobody would ever be able to compare, English urban-industrial working-class life with the life of the 'underprivileged' in the late twentieth century.

In contrast to the 50 cycles stolen in Sunderland in 1938, during 1990 in the Tyne and Wear Fire Brigade area (of which Sunderland constitutes approximately a quarter) there were 1,438 cars not simply stolen, but burnt out, most of them after having been stolen. This was an increase of 1,088 on 1980, when 350 cars were burnt out. Between 1989 and 1990 there was a rise of 49 per cent in cases of arson in the Northumbria police area (Tyne and Wear and Northumberland, of which Sunderland constitutes approximately a fifth).

In 1989 there were 19 cases of murder, in 1990 26, a record number.

In 1989 there were 58 threats to kill, in 1990 112.

In 1906 there had been 3,174 persons tried for burglary in the whole country; in 1990 in the Northumbria police area alone there were 152,000 cases of burglary, theft and robbery known to the police.

The total of reported crime increased in the single year 1989-90 for the single police area of Northumbria by a total in excess of the absolute limits of the variation of the conviction figures during the fifty-year period 1857-1906 for the whole country.[22]

It therefore shows a lack of historical perspective to attribute the rise in the frequency of criminal activities, mainly of young men, to factors which have marginally altered from year to year, or within the period of only a decade.[23]

Notes

1   *Sunderland Echo,* 9 January 1992.

2   *Ibid.,* 14 January 1992.

3   In the form in which it is known in the English language, the Book of Common Prayer originates from Archbishop Cranmer's rendering into English a simplified, reformed, combined version of the medieval Latin service books, which appeared in 1549. Still most familiar are the words of the 1662 version, generally in use for over 200 years and still in use in places today. Marriage was ordained by God 'for the procreation of children, to be brought up in the fear and nurture of the Lord, and to the praise of his holy Name'. Matrimony was therefore 'not by any to be enterprised, nor taken in hand, unadvisedly, lightly, or wantonly, to satisfy man's carnal lusts and appetites, like brute beasts that have no understanding'.

4   Euphemisms are not simply sought for sins. *Mores* is simply the Latin word for morals.

5   Mayhew, P., Elliott, D., and Dowds, L., *The 1988 British Crime Survey, Home Office Research Study 111,* London: HMSO, 1989, p. 22. The survey covered 10,400 households in England and Wales. One adult in each household was interviewed early in 1988. Another such 'victims' survey is not planned until 1993.

6   *Ibid.,* pp. 13-15, 25.

7   'Criminal Careers of Those Born in 1953, 1958 and 1963', Home Office Statistical Bulletin, 32/89, 15 September 1989.

8   Jowell, R. and Airey, C. (eds.), *British Social Attitudes: The 1984 Report*, Aldershot: 1984.

9   Henley Centre for Forecasting, 1992.

10   Jacob, H., and Lineberry, R., Washington, D.C.: Department of Justice, 1982.

11   Home Office, *Criminal Statistics: England and Wales 1906*, London: HMSO, 1908. Home Office, *Criminal Statistics: England and Wales 1990*, Cm 1935, London: HMSO, May 1992. Field, S., *Trends in Crime and Their Interpretation; A Study of Recorded Crime in Post-war England and Wales*, Home Office Research Study 119, London: HMSO, September 1990.

12   *Criminal Statistics 1990*.

13   *Criminal Statistics*, annual volumes.
Population of England and Wales, millions:

1861	20.1;	1871	22.7
1881	26.0;	1891	29.0
1901	32.5		

Indictable offenses reported to the police as committed, number:

1861	88,480;	1871	81,973;
1881	97,105;	1891	79,743;
1901	80,962		

Indictable offenses per 100,000 population:

1861	438;	1871	357;
1881	373;	1891	276;
1901	249		

14   *Ibid.*
Indictable offenses known to the police (later, notifiable offenses recorded by the police, excluding criminal damage under £20): England and Wales:

1938	283,200 (population 41 million)
1985	3,426,400
1989	3,706,200
1990	4,364,000 (population 50 million).

15   *Criminal Statistics*, annual volumes. CSO, *Monthly Digest of Statistics 557*, May 1992, Table 5.1, p. 34. *Criminal Statistics* provide the figures in this section for 1990. The *Monthly Digest of Statistics* the more up-to-date but less detailed figures for 1991.

16   *Criminal Statistics*, annual volumes. *Criminal Statistics 1990*.

17   'There are no crimes and criminals in these days.' 'A Study in Scarlet', *Lippincott's Magazine*, 1887.

18   'The Indictment Against Christianity' (1917), Inge, W.R., *Outspoken Essays*, London: Longman, Green, 1921, p. 245. Emphasis added.

94

19 'The Progress of Crime Since 1857', *Criminal Statistics 1906*, London: HMSO, 1908.

20 *Criminal Statistics 1938*, London: HMSO, 1939.

21 See Daley, H., *This Small Cloud: A Personal Memoir*, London: 1986. It is clear from Daley's account of his experiences that policing the London working-class and its law-breaking fringes in Hammersmith and Wandsworth in his day (1925-50) *was* very much a 'Dixon of Dock Green' affair. Daley, though he never moved out of the other-ranks of the police force, was otherwise an exceptional man. He was a respected intimate of the Bloomsbury Set for his intellectual prowess as well as for his homosexuality. The book is also a good source of information on working-class culture in the fishing communities of East Anglia during his boyhood.

22 19,000, from 171,891 to 190,479 (as compared with the fifty-year spread 1857-1906 from maximum crime rate to minimum crime rate for the whole country of 15,000). *Annual Report of the Chief Constable to the Northumbria Police Authority 1990*, April 1991.

23 When the *Monthly Digest* published the quarterly crime figures in March 1992, the broadsheets issued the usual caveat that they should be treated with caution, that the rise 1990-91 had been forecast by researchers who had established a statistical link between economic recession and rising crime, and reported statements that 'the truly appalling figures were the result of ministerial inactivity', and so forth. 'It is the Home Secretary who should be in the dock', said one senior politician. (*Guardian*, 10 March 1992.)

8

The Causes of Incivility

There is a great deal of emphasis on 'unemployment' as the explanation for the rise in incivility in England in the past three decades. The briefest look at the trend of crime and the trend of unemployment shows that this is incorrect, and that other, quite different forces must be at work.

The earliest fairly usable figures on unemployment appear with the second issue of the Board of Trade's *Labour Gazette* in 1893, when crime figures were low and falling.[1] The only source from which trustworthy, the *Gazette* says 'perfectly trustworthy' unemployment statistics could be obtained were those workmen's organizations which paid out-of-work benefit. The figures, which cover only 308,000 employees, are reliable in themselves, i.e. they give an accurate picture of the trades they cover, but because they deal on the whole with the elite of the labour force at the time they probably considerably understate unemployment overall. National unemployment in May 1893 among the members of the 26 unions that paid unemployment benefit was 6.2 per cent. But in some trades unemployment was much heavier, and employment was not by any means regular. Unemployment among the shipyard workers of Tyne and Wear district, for example, was 32 per cent in March of 1893, and still as high as 18 per cent in May of 1893. In the low crime year of 1911 unemployment was low at 2.5 per cent. (The figures by then covered 767,000 workers.)

But whatever the annual volume and whatever the trend of unemployment, the crime rate remained stable or fell at the end of the nineteenth and the beginning of the twentieth century, rose gradually until the 1960s and then rose rapidly from the 1960s onwards—very rapidly in the late 1970s and the 1980s.

Thus national unemployment stood at 21 per cent in 1931 (the figures now covering the 12.4 million insured workers). In mining 27 per cent, and in shipbuilding and shiprepairing 54 per cent were unemployed. In the large coalmining and shipbuilding town of Sunderland the average rate of unemployment from 1927 to 1934 was 34.6 per cent.[2] These unemployment figures were higher than any experienced in the 1970s or 1980s, and their growth was accompanied by nothing comparable to the crime figures of those later decades. Nationally there were still over a million and half insured people out of work in 1939.

By contrast, there was a period of twenty years, from the mid-fifties to the mid-1970s during which the crime rate rose inexorably, while unemployment was continuously at a low level. Unemployment then rose steadily in the second half of the 1970s, reaching a peak of 12.9 per cent in 1984, falling back to 5.9 per cent in 1990 before rising again—never approaching any closer than that to the figures of the 1930s.

The same pattern is found in the Northern region, at a higher level of unemployment: in the second half of the 1980s crime rose rapidly while unemployment fell from 16.7 per cent in 1985 to 8.7 per cent in 1990 (rising to 10.2 per cent in 1991), male unemployment falling from 19.7 per cent to 11. 6 per cent (rising to 13.7 per cent in April 1991). In April of the high crime year of 1991 there were 9,500 men unemployed in Sunderland, as compared with 14,500 in the November of the by comparison very low, but for the time quite normal, crime year of 1938.[3]

The percentage of Great Britain's population in the labour force rose from 46 per cent in 1971 to 48 per cent in 1985, from 24.9 million to 26.4 million.

Unemployment and crime are of course intimately interconnected. At any level of crime, those who are unemployed are more likely than the employed to have the option of criminal activity brought within the purview of their life-choices. Whatever the unemployment rate, criminals are more likely than non-criminals to eschew conventional employment opportunities. They are more likely to make themselves objectively unattractive to a potential employer. Criminals give their residential area a bad name, and innocent neighbours seeking jobs are stigmatized, suffer from prejudice, because of it—someone from that area is realistically considered *more likely* than someone from another area to be a bad employment risk. We are talking, of course, of 'employment' and 'unemployment' in their modern form in the United Kingdom, with something like the degree and type of compulsion exercised on various people to work, and the material and reputational conditions under which various people have to exist if they are not in employment.

That unemployment is not, and cannot have been one of the main causes for the *growth* of crime in this country is clearly proven by the historical fact that the trend of the overall figures of crime and the overall figures of unemployment bear little relationship to one another. Looking to the future, which exponent of the view that unemployment in itself is a principal cause of contemporary crime levels would be prepared to maintain, however so speculatively, that if the rate of unemployment were to fall to the level of the 1960s, the crime rate would fall to the level of the 1960s? If maintained for a year, what effect would such a theorist say full employment would have on the crime figures? If maintained for five, for ten years?

A powerful phrase was introduced into such discussions as these by the nineteenth-century Swiss historian, Jakob Burckhardt. He wrote of the 'terrible simplifiers' who were likely to have an ever larger and more deleterious effect on civil life. He feared that modern urban populations, while being more anxious to discuss public affairs than rural populations, nevertheless—perhaps even therefore—put themselves with easier reach of simplifying demagogues.[4]

Crime is not the only option open to someone who is unemployed. There is not this single necessary reaction, and this single, simple cause and effect. There is a very large number of possible reactions by the given individual and amongst individuals to unemployment and of fellow-citizens to the manner in which unemployment is personally confronted and coped with.

High unemployment was associated with low criminality in the 1930s. Low unemployment was associated with growing criminality in the 1960s. Unemployment between these two extremes was associated with high and rapidly increasing crime in the mid-1980s. In the early 1990s there was high unemployment and high crime rates.

The difference between the beginning and the end of the twentieth century, in so far as unemployment and crime are concerned, was that British society at the later period was successful in closing off the option of crime as a life style for a far lower proportion of the unemployed than was the case in the 1900s or 1930s. Those who in the 1990s do say, 'And a good thing too, for the working-class has broken out of its former state of wantlessness and servility' do not contradict this point, but illustrate it. Their error is their belief that what they think is desirable, violent and disorderly protest among the young unemployed, is factually inevitable. That is their wishful, not scientific thinking.

What is fundamental is the change in the moral definition of the unemployment situation. The pressures pushing unemployed people into the criminal option, and especially the unemployed young man, have increased, and the pressures towards non-criminal coping have weakened.

Exactly the same point about this phenomenon of 'terrible simplification' can be made more clearly, perhaps, in relation to a less salient matter. When in the early 1990s young English males looted and fire-bombed the small shops in their localities, sometimes starting the proceedings with arson attacks on the common facilities of their neighbours, such as the community association building (as a Hartcliffe, Bristol, 16-17 July 1992), the 'explanation' frequently offered by media discussants was 'boredom', as if between 'boredom' and 'arson' there were no intermediate options. Yet clearly the rich culture—chapels with all their religious and secular activities, football teams, Friendly Societies, cycling clubs, as well as innumerable other formal and informal networks of activity—constituted the prophylactic against boredom that the communities of the respectable English working class built up in the nineteenth and twentieth centuries.

That these options are not available to the bored young of the 1990s is a cultural fact. We do not suggest here to the slightest degree that these extra-familial institutions of the urban-industrial working class either can or ought to be restored. The argument is only this. Other options were available to and utilized by the forebears of the bored looters and arsonists, and looting and arson were very rare among them. This shows that the proposition 'boredom causes riot', like 'unemployment causes crime', is an ahistorical over-simplification.

'Poverty' is also a theory put forward as the explanation for the rise in crime since 1960.

This claim cannot mean poverty as the term would have been understood in the 1930s (or even as late as the 1950s, when social surveys generally showed that working people, and the unemployed and aged no longer felt 'poor'). The chances of obtaining within society's rules adequate and ensured supplies of food, clothing and shelter at any given level of intelligence and dexterity, training, diligence, and good or ill fortune were indisputably worse in the low-crime working-class communities of the second half of the nineteenth and the first half of the twentieth century in this country than in crime-ridden areas today. (Those nineteenth and early-twentieth century British communities were themselves not 'poor' by the standards of law-abiding pre-industrial communities in this country and elsewhere in the world.)

The period of the steepest rises in crime has been a period of unprecedented, and quite possibly historically unrepeatable prosperity, punctuated by momentary pauses or small and very brief declines in the standard of cash-purchaseable living, relatively free from both external and civil war. The simplest overall measure of this is the rise in the Gross Domestic Product (GDP). Indexing 1980 as 100, in real terms the general cash-standard of living in 1961 was only two-thirds of that enjoyed in 1980, and had risen to 110 by 1985. Re-indexing at a much higher standard of living, taking 1985 as 100, the cash-standard of living had risen from 90 in 1981 to 117 by 1990. At 1985 prices the GDP was £319 billion in 1981, and £417 billion in 1990. Recessions on the scale experienced since the Second World War had simply set the cash standard of living back to what it had been about two years before.

Nothing proves prosperity more than life itself. In 1901 a man's expectation of life at birth in the United Kingdom was 48; in 1981 it was 70. In 1901 the expectation of life for a woman was 52; in 1981 it was 76. In England and Wales in 1981 a 65-year-old man had a life expectancy of a further 13 years, by 1988 this had increased to 14 years. The life expectancy of a 65-year-old woman had been 13 years in 1931; it was 17 years in 1981 and had risen to 18 years by 1988.[5] The significance of this is not diminished by the fact that it is no cause for complacency about those of all ages who are still stricken by fatal diseases. (Nor does it diminish the obligation to lead a life as likely as possible to retain and heighten personal vitality, so that a person not stricken by fate is not only no burden to others, but has the surplus energy to use for their benefit.)

The sense that things had been gradually improving materially was widespread. In 1984 1,700 people were asked to say what their parents' class had been, and what their own class was. 67 per cent said that their parents had been either 'poor' or 'working class' (8 per cent and 59 per cent respectively), but only 51 per cent said they were poor or working class (3 per cent and 48 per cent).[6]

The poorest had at worst *almost* proportionately shared in these improvements, at least to the extent that their absolute claim to the standard of living *purchaseable with cash* was higher .

In 1938, in his influential up-dating of the *Communist Manifesto* of ninety years before, Leon Trotsky reaffirmed that the strategic task of communists lay 'not in reforming capitalism but its overthrow'. Prior to the revolution of the armed proletariat it was necessary to progressively weaken the forces sustaining the law and order of the capitalist State. Trotsky's so-called 'transitional programme' described various tactics for doing this. Their common feature was that, first, they were all demands made in the name of 'bourgeois justice' on the 'bourgeois State' and, second, that they could not possibly be met by bourgeois society. The essence of the system of transitional demands was that ever more openly and decisively they would be directed against 'the very foundations of the bourgeois regime'.

When Trotsky was writing he took it for granted that one of the best destabilizing demands, the (to Trotsky) patent unrealizability of which would lead the workers to 'understand the necessity of liquidating capitalist slavery', was that wages and social benefits should be required to keep pace with inflation.[7]

For most of the twenty years of rapid increase in crime rates 1970-90 it was, on the contrary, taken for granted by the bourgeois parties of the right and the left that wages and social benefits should not merely keep pace with inflation, but that it was a serious indictment of the system if real growth did not take place, not only in the overall standard of living, but in the standard of living of all sections of the population considered separately.

It was only in the late 1980s that 'Thatcherism' succeeded in a few instances in cutting the link between inflation and welfare payments. In one notable instance, welfare payments for young people who were deemed to be living at home, there was a drastic cut in the standard of living of those who were not in fact living at home. In so far as the latter resorted to criminal activities, the theorists of 'poverty' in the plain sense at last had cases at which they could point and could say, 'crimes are due to poverty, this young man is poor, therefore he has committed a crime'. At least their minor premise now had at any rate some empirical support.

For most of the period during which the frequency of recorded crimes was rapidly increasing, 'poverty', if it were also to be increasing (as it had to be to keep the connection with crime) had to carry a specialized meaning if the theory were to be kept intact.

In its most general form (whatever the justification may or may not be of widening the word 'poverty' to describe it) the notion of 'relative deprivation' is powerful and all-embracing to the point of being tautological.

The theory of relative deprivation merely states that what is crucial as the experience of 'poverty' is not the absolute quantity of beneficial experiences enjoyed or potentially claimable by a person (cash goods and services, power, prestige, affection, or whatever the person values), but the quantity to which the person feels entitled.

It has equal utility in explaining the petty crime of a shoplifter in Woolworths, an infant's temper tantrums, the conduct of a corrupt businessman or banker in his office suite, a ram-raider smashing into a High Street shop front, or the atrocities of any tyrant, ancient or modern.

In the 1920s and 1930s, in spite of the fact that a victorious Germany was unlikely to have been magnanimous to the vanquished, Hitler secured a great deal of support not only in Germany but abroad for his claim that the German people were entitled not to pay reparations, entitled to rule in Alsace-Lorraine, entitled as a people to as generous living space in Eastern Europe as France enjoyed with her imperial possessions,[8] entitled to be treated as equals in the community of nations and not to be the sole bearers with their allies of war guilt, and so on.

The theory of relative deprivation when applied to crime states that the *gap* between legitimate (felt-to-be-legitimate) expectations and their fulfilment is the measure of grievance, and grievance is the cause of law-breaking.

As important to the theory as the width of the gap is the strength of the sense of entitlement—the strength of the feelings of anger when expectations are not fully met. If law-breaking is to be encouraged it is essential, on this view, that it must be someone else, or some system, that is to blame for the existence of the gap. Successful attribution of fault to others, and therefore a clear conscience for oneself, depends upon a belief in what Fraser in a famous passage called the transference of evil. It is technically possible for a person to rid, and morally (or more likely amorally) he is justified in ridding himself of some unpleasant condition onto someone else. Fraser gives several striking examples of the more or less ruthless or naive attempts by the sufferer and his theoretical supporters (e.g., witch doctors, witches), based upon this superstition, to transfer to others conditions existing in the life of the 'cunning and selfish' transferrer.[9]

The actual standard of living can therefore be rising rapidly, but if expectations of the standard of living to which people are entitled are rising even more rapidly, then not satisfaction, but discontent is being created.

The leading characteristic of successful urban-industrial societies so far has been their capacity to produce in abundance goods and services that can be distributed in accordance with cash claims to them. But producing such marketable goods and services is necessarily more difficult than producing the wish to possess them. Urban-industrial societies have therefore been even more successful in producing expectations of entitlement to riches than producing the riches themselves. They are adept above all, that is, in producing relative deprivation.

The link between high levels of relative deprivation and *prosperity* is quite clear in the case of white-collar crime, and as there are no political gains to be made by denying it, the link is not disputed. Galbraith has applied the theory of high prosperity and high white-collar crime rates to embezzlement in particular. However much money they have, there are always people who feel that they need more. In good times money is plentiful and people are, on the one hand, relaxed and trusting and, on the other, some feel they could make better use of the money for personal or business purposes than the fools and crooks that have it and do not deserve it. In a depression all this is reversed. Money is watched with a narrow, suspicious eye. Audits are penetrating and meticulous. The crooked businessman adjusts his greed to bring it within the narrowed limits of what he can get away with. 'Commercial morality enormously improves.'[10]

The businessman not only himself experiences, for commercial reasons he also engenders relative deprivation—he heightens the customer's yearning for and feeling of entitlement to more saleable goods than the customer can actually afford. The *Guardian* journalist fosters it for reasons of social justice. The Trotskyist fosters it for reasons of revolutionary strategy.

The entrepreneur uses commercial advertising to heighten feelings of relative deprivation. The social reformer and revolutionary must find other means of accomplishing in essence the same objective. One of their favoured devices is to measure relative deprivation as the gap between the richest and poorest in the society, and call the wideness of this gap the degree of poverty.[11] The wider the gap, the greater the relative deprivation, the more severe the poverty. So long as the gap between the richest and the poorest is as wide or widens, the theory of 'poverty' as the cause of crime is then quite immune from any rise in the standard of living of the poor, no matter how large that rise may be.

While it has its merits and effects, the device has three flaws. One is that the gap between rich and poor cannot be relied on always to widen. The second is that the gap between rich and poor, in what they wore, in household equipment, in having servants or being servants, in means of transport, in manner of speech, was much more obvious before, say, the First World War when crime rates were falling than it is today when crime rates are rising. The third is that though the theory requires rises in crime to be proportionate to rate of the widening of the gap between rich and poor, people in poverty cannot be relied upon themselves to perceive that the gap is widening. The gap will be obvious enough, but the rate at which the gap is widening will not necessarily be sufficiently perceptible to the ordinary man or woman in the street. He or she will have to be told about it, and the social reformer does not always have the resources to communicate the message effectively in the face of disagreement even among professionals about the facts.

A much more successful device, with far fewer defects, through which feelings of relative deprivation can be created and maintained at a high level and the cause of social justice assisted is that of securing widespread agreement that the 'poverty line' should be fixed at some percentage point above the level of the State welfare benefit. For, if a person is 'in poverty' when his or her income is less than, say, 140 per cent of the welfare benefit level, then raising the State welfare benefit does not reduce the number of people in poverty, but increases it. It is a fail-safe mechanism, put positively, for the constant re-creation of pressure for the improvement of the lot of the poorest or, put negatively, for the constant re-creation of discontent.[12]

Notes

1 Board of Trade, *The Labour Gazette*, 1, 2, June 1893, and monthly thereafter, changing its name from time to time (in 1991 the Department of Employment, *Employment Gazette*).

2 Report of an Investigation into Maternal Mortality, Cd.5422, London: HMSO, 1937.

3   *Ibid.*, and *Ministry of Labour Gazette*, 46, December 1938. The 1991 figures for 'Sunderland North' and 'Sunderland South' correspond to the 'Sunderland' figure for 1938.

4   Burckhardt, J., *Reflections on History* (1905), London: Allen and Unwin, 1943, p. 144.

5   *Population Trends 66*, OPCS, Winter 1991

6   *British Social Attitudes* 1984.

7   Trotsky, L., *The Death Agony of Capitalism and the Tasks of the Fourth International* (also referred to as the *Transitional Programme*) (1938), London: The Other Press, 1979, pp. 10-12.

Trotsky took the idea of the destabilizing effect on society of making impossible demands on its capacity to meet them from Marx and Engels. That had written that if the bourgeoisie agreed to nationalize the railways and the factories, 'the workers must demand that these ... shall be simply confiscated'. If the bourgeoisie agreed to the taxation of the rich, the communists must demand proportional taxation. If the bourgeoisie agreed to proportional taxation, communists must demand progressive taxation. If the bourgeoisie agreed to progressive taxation, the communists must demand crippling progressive taxation'. 'Address of the Central Committee to the Communist League' (1850), in Marx, K., and Engels, F., *Selected Works*, I, Moscow: Foreign Languages Publishing House, 1958, p. 116.

8   See, for example, 'Der Kampf um den deutschen Lebensraum', *Völkischer Beobachter*, 19 January 1929. This article is cast exactly on the model of 'relative deprivation'. On the one side there was the gap between the lebensraum of 'poor' Germany and the lebensraum of the 'rich' Western nations. On the other side there were easier 'marks' who could be plundered to make up the difference. On the basis of righteous anger, among other consequences demanded was driving the Poles out of Poland, back to the Asia where they came from to usurp it. This would free the land for the Germans who were really entitled to it. The 'spiritually poor' Poles, a people 'without intelligence', 'gifted only in the arts of sharp-dealing', dirty and lazy, who had time after time shown their unlimited incapacity at state-building, could then on their retreat to Asia do their usual thing, get drunk on hard spirits, before they froze to death in the Russian cold—and much of the same. Relative deprivation's vagueness and generality of application means that its usefulness as a propaganda tool is not by any means limited to the interests of 'the poor'.

9   Fraser, J.G., *The Golden Bough* (1922), London: Macmillan, 1963, pp. 706-07 and 711-13.

10 Galbraith, J.K., *The Great Crash, 1929*, London: Hamish Hamilton. The boom of the 1980s worldwide was one of the biggest and longest in history. It was also the decade in which both the scale and rate of business scandal were at their greatest.

11　'Mr. Field said that some of his constituents were without hope because ... "While the average standard of living has increased, under the steward-ship of this government, the poor have seen the very smallest increase".' *The Times*, 24 January 1992.

12　Michael Meacher, the shadow Secretary of State for the Social Services, said that the government was 'wilfully impoverishing the poor part of the population and claimed that *more than ten million* people live below the poverty line'. *The Times*, 24 January 1992.

9

The Intellectuals' New Betrayal

Discontent can be minimal at a low and even with (as during, say the Second World War) a declining standard of living if a population is socialized to expect nothing but a low standard of living. The low crime figures of the period prior to the Great War was clearly associated with not only the indigenous working-class culture of neighbourhood, workplace, Friendly Society, political party and Trade Union, but also the resources of propaganda that were devoted to inculcating into the working-class, on the one hand low expectations of values that can be only realised through the possession and expenditure of money, and on the other hand high expectations of non-cash values.

Such values are found throughout the Introduction to the New Code of 1904 for the elementary schools of England and Wales, thought to have been written by J.W. Mackail, sometime Professor of Poetry at the University of Oxford:

> Though their opportunities are but brief, the teachers can yet do much to lay the foundations of conduct. They can endeavour, by example and influence, aided by a sense of discipline, which should pervade the School, to implant in the children habits of industry, self-control, and courageous perseverance in the face of difficulties; they can teach them to reverence what is noble, to be ready for self-sacrifice, and to strive their utmost after purity and truth; they can foster a strong respect for duty, and that consideration and respect for others which must be the foundation of unselfishness and the true basis for all good manners; while the corporate life of the School, especially in the playground, should develop that instinct for fair-play and loyalty to one another which is the germ of a wider sense of honour in later life. In all these endeavours the School should enlist, as far as possible, the interest and co-operation of the parents and home in a united effort to enable the

children not merely to reach their full development as individuals, but also to become upright and useful members of the community in which they live, and worthy sons and daughters of the country to which they belong'.[1]

... and much more of the same.

Leicester University's Labour Market Study Group compared jobless 18-24-year-olds in Sunderland, St Albans, Leicester and Stafford.[2] It reported that a new 'culture' was growing up in Sunderland. Among school children it takes the form of regarding working for O- or A-levels as a senseless activity, 'because they have seen their mates who have worked hard ending up in the same position with no prospect of a job'.

Much the same attitude prevails towards government training courses. These values, the dissenting hopelessness of a fragmented but uniform mass, were opening celebrated through the main media of communication in this country for the first time in the commercially successful song of the group 'Pink Floyd':

We don't need no education
We don't need no thought control
No dark sarcasm in the classroom
Teachers leave the kids alone ...
All in all
You're just another brick in the wall.[3]

'Almost any means of getting extra cash, legal or otherwise, was becoming regarded as acceptable in whole communities.'[4]

'Culture' and 'whole communities' in this context are both terms to be treated with caution. What exists is an aggregate of people sharing a similar life style characterized by a relatively high degree of *alienation* from the notion that the interests of each individual should be adjusted to those of others. By the early 1990s young unemployed males merely showed this phenomenon to a high degree. 'Market' societies such those of the West, and perhaps in the future those of former communist societies,[5] tend to expand this element in all personalities and institutions. In certain places and people this alienation exceeds the average and spills over into anti-social behaviour *some of which is quite likely both to be defined as such by most people, and to be highly visible to the victim* (burglary, theft, destruction and defacement). In the past twenty or thirty years in this country this spilling-over has taken place predominantly among those in the later years of compulsory schooling and the few years after that; and among males, but with females catching up on them.[6]

They reject not only the dominant culture, but any view that their own attitudes and conduct should be governed either by the way they are 'fetched up' or by the way in which they are praised or blamed, rewarded or punished according to the correspondence of their conduct to the highest standards of the surrounding acculturated, and therefore to be despised, population.

There can be a uniform and mass response of individuals to a given situation, without that response being a cultural response. Such a uniform response where the cultural features are weak may be quiescent. Where pure materialism sets in, Lawrence wrote,

> the soul is automatically pivoted, and the most diverse creatures fall into a common mechanical unison. ... It is not a homogeneous, spontaneous coherence so much as a disintegrated amorphousness which lends itself to perfect mechanical unison.[7]

Or it may be a non-cultural response of general disorder, such as Hannah Arendt describes as the state of affairs out of which grew the totalitarian regimes of twentieth-century Europe. The origins of totalitarianism lay, she argues, in 'one great unorganized mass of furious individuals' who had nothing in common except their apprehension that the most respected and representative articulators of the existing culture were fools, and the elected holders of public office were fraudulent. Their 'self-centred bitterness, though repeated again and again in individual isolation, was not a common bond despite its tendency to extinguish individual differences', and this very self-centredness 'went hand-in-hand with a decisive weakening of the instinct for self-preservation'.[8]

Similarly, a culture may be harmonious with that of another, as those of the nations of Western Europe became after 1945, or in conflict with it, as when the strong cultures of England and Germany clashed in the 1914-18 war. Particular sections within a state can form cultures which are either consensual with or in opposition to the dominant culture, as the culture of English mining communities were distinct but consensual at one time (the Durham Light Infantry raised more volunteer battalions during the 1914-18 war than any other regiment, mainly composed of miners) and in conflict at another (as when Marxian views of the world gained ground in the 1970s and 1980s).

Whether any particular culture is better or worse than any particular state of either acquiescent *anomie* or temporary, transitional generalized, 'necessary' violence is therefore a crucial even though a separate matter. Obviously, the Nazi movement 1920-45 was a major example of a strong culture, as were the many explicitly culture-building *volkisch* organizations that prepared the way for it, with their strong and shared beliefs about the 'facts' of ineradicable racial superiority and inferiority, and the about the moral decadence of city life as compared with life in the village and small town.

The cultural elements of socialization and social control in the situation described by the Leicester group are present but minimal. Culture implies the successful inculcation of reverence for the standards of the group, even if the group is the Mafia family. The 'culture' of negation is essentially a culture of irreverence.

Culture implies the virtue of conformity to social rules. Activities may in practice take the form of a more-or-less uniform following of fashion, with marginal differentiation into imitators of one or another style of dress, music and 'politics' of commercially successful musical performers (in the early 1990s followers of, for example, 'hard core' groups such as 'Napalm Death' or 'rap' groups such as 'Public Enemy'). But such a 'culture' of alienation essentially legitimizes the fashion in terms of isolated nonconformity or imagined counter-conformity.[9]

Culture implies that those areas of life defined as central to its maintenance are protected by a sense of the sacred. The 'culture' of alienation is characterized by an obsession to uncover the 'holy' so that it can be turned to ridicule, and to hunt out of any 'sacred' areas that remain, in order to have a vehicle for its entertaining profanities.[10]

'Cultural' exemplars in this situation are those who are boldest in defiance, negation, irreverence, non-conformity, and profanity towards residual rule-bound, other-regarding restraints. Such acculturation and peer group pressure as do exist are directed towards encouraging the growth of hostility to both socialization and social control, and fostering the notion that everyone must 'do her own thing'. Peer-group hostility, that is, is directed only against those who attempt to 'improve themselves' by using the facilities of education, training and recreation deemed effective for that purpose by 'respectable' society: one is free to *fail* to improve oneself in a wide variety of ways.

Certainly assisted by outside definers of their situation, each such person, to the extent that she lies towards the 'alienated' end of the spectrum, interprets the existing culture (including that of school, and of training and employment opportunities) as intrinsically useless, avoidably unjust, and a principal cause of her own failure. In its consequences for anti-social reactions to the situation, this is at the opposite pole to the world-view that everybody's lot, to the end of their days, from which there is no escape, is to 'suffer and endure'. No art, no force, can free humankind from that.[11]

Those who wish to continue to use the word 'culture' to describe a situation of *anomie*—of many alienated people sharing and sanctioning the *absence* of socially-oriented values—are, of course, perfectly free to do so.

Those who come most thoroughly to accept the definition of the situation that 'life' is about immediate and self-regarding enjoyment, and that insurmountable and irremovable obstacles to enjoyment are illegitimately erected by outside enemies and that therefore they owe other people nothing, are inevitably the young people most frequently recruited to the ranks of the unemployed.

As the Leicester study points out, one in three of the Sunderland sample had never experienced full-time employment. But children from the same council estates had different educational aspirations and employment successes, depending upon the extent to which they had accepted this culture of alienation as their own. In 1991 the academically most successful sets of pupils, drawn from across the town's spectrum of classes and residential areas, were all 'backward' in cultural terms—the most culturally backward, Catholic girls, being the most successful.

Ninety-two per cent of the pupils in the Catholic girls comprehensive school earned five or more GCSEs. In the town's school with the lowest results, a large comprehensive school on a council housing estate, the figure was exactly half that, 46 per cent, and for the boys only, 40 per cent.

At the school with the best examination record, 54 per cent of those with five or more GCSE successes gained A-C grades. At the school with the worst, less than a fifth of that, 10 per cent; and one-quarter of its GCSE candidates failed to pass in even one subject.[12] 'The head teacher ... blamed the problem on absenteeism by pupils.'[13]

Whether at the best or worst schools, those pupils who had resisted the pressures to define school as 'pointless' most successfully—most successfully resisted the notion that this, that, and everything is 'crap'—were those best equipped for success in the short as well as in the long term.

Culture refers to the totality of learned experiences passed from one generation to the next. *Anomie* refers to a state of affairs in which culture is feeble or absent—when every individual responds to a given situation according to his own emotional or his own more-or-less carefully calculated response—when every man does what is right in his own eyes.

The degree of anomic violence, or alternatively the strength of a culture of violence, are both closely connected to the ineffectiveness of the violence of the State. *Anomie* cannot restrain, and an extra-legal culture of violence honours the use of private physical force in the settlement of grievances.

The Anomie of Fatherlessness

In the mid-1960s England was still a society in which anomic, non-cultural resort to extra-legal violence, an overall culture, and sub-cultures of extra-legal violence all remained weak—it was still a peaceable place.

In the autumn of 1991 the rioting took place on Tyneside which received world-wide publicity—and which occasioned this essay. Two youths were killed when, being pursued by the police, they crashed a car they had stolen for a ram-raiding burglary. Their peers living on the estate where the younger of the two lived, Meadow Well, put their neighbours' houses and shops to the torch. These young men, terrorizing the old and the weak in their neighbourhoods with riot and arson, as they normally blighted their lives with the fear and fact of burglary and abuse, were neither immigrants nor the victims of racial prejudice. They were the sons, grandsons and great-grandsons of people who had defined their objectively much worse situation in an entirely different way.

The riot areas were characterized just as much by the statistical deficiency of stable families as they were by a statistical excess of the long-term unemployed. Effective pressure-group propaganda meant that this point was rarely raised publicly.

In one sense the riots were not at all unusual. Similar events had been occurring on a scattered but persistent, widespread and rapidly growing scale. Every Friday and Saturday evening youths crowded into the bars, night clubs, discos, and fast-food places, exclusively designed for a youth clientele, and turned the atmosphere of the town centres into one of nihilistic hedonism, where random physical violence, destruction and defacement of property, and attacks on the police, from being rare up to fifteen years before, had become completely commonplace. Drunk young men now openly urinated in a town's main street. Drunk young women still had at least the residual civility to publicly urinate in the back lanes.

The rioters themselves only claimed that the occasion for the riot was their indignation about the police pursuit of their ram-raiding friends. (Graffiti on the estate after the riots: 'ramraids revenge'; 'police are murders'; 'Dale Colin we no the score we haven't started yet'; 'Tyson you coul'd'nt catch a cold never mind a ram raider'; 'Pc Coombes you are next Ha Ha'.) That did not prevent them targeting their anger on the one set of people who were conspicuous for their hard work, family-centredness, and modest economic success—the Asian immigrants on the estate. Ashsak Ahmed owned the fish and chip shop: the business and his home were both attacked. Nachter Rai, the newsagent, found that a mob of fifty looters had broken in while she slept. She, her husband, and their two children escaped only with the clothes they were able to put on. As a result of their treatment by the rioters, all ten Asian families left the estate to start again elsewhere.[14]

Above a certain level of material constraint, the definition of the situation becomes the prime determinant of action. Who can effectively mould a person's definition of the situation is the master of his life. To use Marxist phraseology, but to contradict Marxist doctrine, in rich societies the control of the means of mental production, either to foster *anomie* or to support cultural standards of conflict or consensus, become at least as important as the control of the means of material production.

To reach a wide audience, and especially to reach from Los Angeles to Tyneside, from Los Angeles to Berlin and Moscow, the activity of major capitalist communicators like Time-Warner is required. In the early 1990s Time-Warner was quite willing to make and sell a rap singer's song in which the murder of policemen was celebrated. Ice-T's 'Cop Killer' included such lines as 'I'm 'bout to dust some cops off', and 'Die, pig, die'. (Another song on the same album, 'KKK Bitch', made sexual references to the 12-year-old niece of the Democratic party's 1992 candidate for the vice-presidency of the United States.) The head of Time-Warner, Gerald Levin, justified the making and marketing of the album in terms of his onerous yet clear public duty. Time-Warner 'must help ensure that the voices of the powerless, the disenfranchised, those at the margins, are heard'. 'Cop Killer' was, he said, 'a shout of pain and protest'.[15]

That there was an element of perceived public duty is suggested by the likelihood that, even if it would have sold, Time-Warner would have refused to give world-wide circulation to a song called 'Drug-pusher Killer' from equally powerless and disenfranchised neighbours that said 'I'm 'bout to dust some vandals off', or 'Die, thief, die'.

Not every message of the powerless is given an effective voice by the powerful who control the means of communication. When effective community self-protection breaks down, very large numbers of the old and poor who are powerless would rather have police protection than be subject to the depredations in their own lives of 'disenfranchised' (whatever Levin meant by this in this context) young men. But boring messages of common sense and decency from the powerless reap meagre and uncertain profits; and, very frequently in the media, the common sense and decency of the powerless cease to be boring only when they are available to be mocked.

The question is, to whom is the megaphone handed, and why? Those who control the main media of modern communication are motivated by the desire for monetary gain, as well by the highly developed sense of civic obligation of companies like Time-Warner, and therefore will amplify messages which will sell in the market niches they can discover. If incitement to incivility and worse sells better than its opposite, even to populations that formerly protected themselves fiercely against the expansion of the elements in everyone's personality to which destruction and disorder appeal, then incivility will be propagated for profit.

The rioters objectively enjoyed unprecedentedly secure and variegated supply of food, drink and clothing, with access to doctors and hospitals, superior to anything that existed before they were born, with ready access to places of entertainment and education (many public facilities such as night schools, swimming baths and local authority entertainment complexes are free always or at certain times to the unemployed). They rioted because of their poverty.

No doubt crime and riot are 'connected with' current English levels of poverty. If people riot because they think they are poor, then the connection is there. But Anglicans of Bangladesh and Uganda must have been astonished to hear the Archbishop of Canterbury suggest at all, in context or out of context, that the Welfare State had so lamentably failed the English.

They rioted because of their 'poor housing'. The rioters lived neither in tower blocks nor, in anything but a very strained sense of the term, in the inner city. Those who lived on the riot estate lived in post-war semi-detached houses with gardens. Meadow Well is bordered on the east by open park land, and laid out in at any rate a local authority's genuine attempt at garden city principles. In most cases housing was free, being paid for through housing benefit. The most striking thing about the dwellings is the large number whose roofs have been stripped of their slates, leaving the rest of the structure open to the ravages of the weather. They have been taken by thieves for the few pence each slate brings as stolen property.

For decades the estate had been the beneficiary of virtually every social service agency and every central government and local authority grant and initiative. It was one of the first areas to have nursery classes to ensure a head start at school. It would be a daunting but interesting task to attempt to trace and unravel the per capita public expenditure on the estate since, say, 1970, up to and including the local authority and central government 'initiative' in place just when the riot took place. One of the main development projects of the Tyne and Wear Development Corporation lay just over 500 metres from the centre of the estate. The youths rioted because they were 'deprived'.

In a society with every conceivable variety of sports, athletics and outdoor sports' clubs; public service organizations like the St. John's Ambulance Brigade; and self-improvement facilities in the nearby Open Learning Centre, the local libraries, schools and colleges, they rioted because they 'had nothing to do' and they were 'bored'.

With 87 per cent of Tyneside's working population employed, even at the 'depths of a recession' in late 1991, and with a higher proportion of the adult population in work than ever before they rioted because of 'unemployment'. The estate had access to the labour market of the whole of Tyneside. Smith's Park, a station of Tyneside's famed rapid transit Metro system, is right in the middle of the estate. (It was always heavily vandalized and quickly re-vandalized.)

The rioters' predecessors lived, objectively, in far inferior conditions of insecurity of employment, shortage of jobs, poverty, and ill-equipped, overcrowded housing. There is not a single incidence of their having deliberately started fires, with the sole purpose of ambushing the firemen called to the scene, and attacking them with stones and bottles. They never slashed firemen's hoses, nor damaged their appliances.[16]

'Unemployment' was indeed the key to the Tyneside riots of 1991. But not unemployment in the sense of the absence of opportunities to work as a paid employee in a drudging job (much less remunerative and exciting than crime).

It was unemployment in the sense of the weakening or complete disappearance of the expectation that a young man should prepare himself for the larger employment to which a job is merely instrumental. This is his employment for a lifetime in a partnership of mutual support of a mature man and a mature woman. It is employment in a years' long commitment to nurturing and socializing until his child is in turn able to earn its own living and raise its own family. Their fathers and grandfathers called their house 'home', and their wife 'our lass'. The sons call their female partner 'the bitch', and their woman's house 'the kennel': 'the bitch is in the kennel'.[17] A nationally exhibited film was made about Meadow Well, 'Dream On', from the point of view of women on the estate. Many of the cast were Meadow Well residents.[18] Discussing its release on the BBC Radio 4 'Today' programme, one of the participating local women said that it correctly portrayed the Meadow-Well male as 'selfish, violent and weak'.[19]

For it was not only or even mainly that the rioters as children were themselves the first or second generation of a home and local life that has left them on average worse off educationally and in social skills than their contemporaries from stable two-parent homes in the same area and in equally deprived working-class homes elsewhere on Tyneside and Wearside. As youths (some themselves the product of single-parent homes, some not) they did not have a taken-for-granted project for life of responsibility for their own wife and children. Their expectations had ceased to be automatically geared to unavoidable parenthood.

To the extent that they are victims of their environment, they are victims of their cultural environment. They are the victims of various ad hoc combinations of destabilizing Marxism whose long march through the institutions began and ended in the family, altruistic anarchism, hedonistic nihilism and *nostalgie de la boue* which excited the undergraduates of 1968 and which until recently were the stock-in-trade of serious journalism.

Critical theory, the New Criminology and various versions of Trotskyism were for a time actually dominant in sociology. Discredited in political and economic life, the 'spirit of sixty-eight' lives on only in the weakening of the link between sex, procreation, child-care, child-rearing, and loyalty in the life-long provision on a non-commercial basis of mutual care within a common place of residence.

In the aftermath of the triumph of Lenin and Mussolini the French essayist Julien Benda published a little book that was widely noticed at the time, but is now remembered only for its title, *La Trahison des clercs*, the intellectuals' betrayal.[20] Instead of loyalty to telling the truth to the best of their ability, they had become advocates of their own 'good causes'. In their 'desire to abase the values of knowledge before the values of action' they had exchanged their scientific integrity for the visionary future of either Bolshevism or Fascism.

There was a second betrayal by the intellectuals when in great numbers they followed the fashion in the 1960s and uncritically acclaimed the then current ideology of town planning. All British cities, and many other European cities, now carry the legacy. The planners eventually faced widespread and successful opposition from the potential victims of housing clearances.

The third betrayal by the intellectuals has lain not so much in their often self-centred celebration of the family's dismantlement, and their unremitting attack since the 1960s on all the taboos that protected family life, as in their wanton ignorance of, or open hostility to the known facts.

Benda's work was based on his recognition of the fragility of civilized values. 'If humanity loses this jewel there is not much chance of finding it again.'[21] The achievement of a humane, free, rich, improving, unified and stable society, is envisaged by ethical capitalists like Adam Smith and Hayek, who are sceptical of State intervention. The same goals are envisaged by ethical socialists like Cobbett, Hobhouse, Orwell, T.H. Marshall and Tawney,[22] for whom the State creates and is sustained by the service to others of self-reliant, self-improving citizens. They agree on this. The creation and the maintenance of such a society depend upon the existence and successful adaptation of an infinitude of benign institutions and of innumerable personal decisions in all the details of everyday life, most of them totally beyond the knowledge of today's social science. Hayek calls them 'spontaneous institutions'. We have called them here 'common sense'.

Societies can decay from within, as well as succumb to external shocks. In many cases, we only know that some things seem to have worked to preserve widespread wealth and harmony, and some destroy it.

Apparently civilized societies have suddenly experienced internecine and international wars, civil strife, totalitarian tyranny and genocidal massacres. These experiences reach so nearly into the recent past, and have continued to spring to life so unexpectedly in one form or another, that it was by no means ridiculous for Horkheimer and Adorno to say that 'the fully enlightened world radiates disaster triumphant'.[23] To those who do not suffer from historical amnesia these words serve as our own society's perpetual *memento mori*.

Notes

1 Introduction to the New Code of the Public Elementary School, 1904, in Maclure, J.S. (ed.), *Educational Documents: England Wales 1816-1967*, London: Methuen, 1968, p. 155.

2 Ashton, D.N., Maguire, M.J., and others, *Young Adults in the Labour Market*, Research Paper No. 55, London: Department of the Environment, 1987.

3 Pink Floyd's 'The Wall' and Jethro Tull's 'Thick as a Brick' were the first successful attempts—because they now were marketable to their young audiences—to portray school as part of the system that crushes the life out of the individual. (Street, J., *Rebel Rock: The Politics of Popular Music*, Oxford: Basil Blackwell, 1986, p. 207.) Such sentiments had been presaged in the 1960s by, for example, 'The Who', and Townsend's line 'hope I die before I grow old' is well known. But 'Another Brick in the Wall' was notable both in openly siding with those who attacked the pathetic conforming, striving "ear 'oles" (see Willis, P., *Learning to Labour*) who paid attention to what school had to teach, and in being a best seller of its time. The song was most frequently heard on radio and television at the end of 1979 and the beginning of 1980—much more frequently, that is, than messages about the vice of premature despair and the virtue of self-improvement which, being neither novel nor shocking, have a very low entertainment value. There is no attempt to reproduce in print the exaggeratedly 'proletarian'

diction. By comparison, their equivalents ten years later made 'Another Brick in the Wall' look like a seriously-intended song of social protest, and Pink Floyd a staid group with a mission of political reform. (In July 1990, the group did indeed take part in a famous anti-wall concert in Berlin's Potsdamer Platz, which in the form of an eight-million dollar televised video event, described by *Select*, October 1990, as 'bombastic, violent and alienating', reached audiences world-wide.)

4   David Ashton, in an interview reported in *The Times*, 26 January 1987. The culture of thieving of the 18-24-year-old 'kids' is modified, according to Mr. Ashton, by the consideration that theft 'does not hurt your own'. But if that 'rule' is anything but verbal, the adherents of the 'culture' reported by Mr. Ashton interpret 'their own' in a very narrow way, which certainly excludes most of their neighbours, whose dwellings and of course shops and other businesses are very unsafe from them.

5   'The number of crimes is rapidly climbing in the new Länder; criminality has not yet reached the proportions, however, of what is normal in West Germany.' »Kriminalität in Sachsen-Anhalt nimmt zu«, *Frankfurter Allgemeine Zeitung*, 29 February 1992.

6   Smoking can be taken as an indication of this. Adult smoking was once a highly sociable activity. It used not to be thought at all curious that cigarette manufacturers should hold royal warrants. But it played incidently an important role as a gender-differentiator, and as a rite de passage to male adulthood. Pre-mature smoking was therefore available to the young and to women as a minor gesture of rebellion against society's norms, and available to women as an assertion of equality with men. But in the 1970s and 1980s it came to be the very type of consumption that was both personally imprudent and costly to fellow-citizens. While its purely pleasurable and social uses continued to be of some importance, comparatively its role as a gesture of defiance was enhanced. The striking thing about smoking, therefore, was that while the proportion of all people smoking was declining, the gap between the proportion of women and men almost disappeared by the end of the 1980s, and young female smokers came to outnumber young male smokers (22 per cent of English women aged 15-24, 17 per cent of men). (Amos, A. and Bostock, Y., *British Medical Journal*, January 1992.)

7   Lawrence, D.H., 'Democracy' (1936), *Selected Essays*, Harmondsworth: Penguin, 1950, p. 94.

8   Arendt, H., *The Origins of Totalitarianism* (1951), New York: Meridian, 1958, p. 315.

9   'Carcass', 'Bolt Thrower', 'Hellbastard' and 'Godflesh' were the names of other hardcore (or 'thrash metal', 'speed metal', or 'death') groups. In 1989 the BBC's arts programme 'Arena' screened a 'Heavy Metal Special'. Finding ways of shocking the bourgeoisie became harder day by day, but you had to

you had to do your best with the limited materials for shocking anybody that were still available. Running out of shockable people, the fly-posters of the group called 'Cult', showing a bearded and long-haired young man as Jesus Christ, with a wreath of razor wire round his head in place of his crown of thorns, but with the empty eyes of a terrorist and pointing a pistol at the reader of the poster, were pasted ... outside the Scripture Union Bookshop. (City of Sunderland, February 1992.) The *isolating* intentions and effects of such a 'culture' is the most obvious impression created for the observer of the crowds of young men, each with his health drink and Ecstasy pill or other drug, wrapped up hour upon hour in his own solitary air-guitarring 'dance'. But the scapegoating potential of such a culture was also being realized and recognized by the early 1990s. The Anti-Defamation League of B'nai B'rith warned that many rock and rap songs had anti-semitic and other racist texts. For example, 'Guns and Roses' recommended the spreading of disease among immigrants and homosexuals; 'Public Enemy' had revived the notion that the Jews were collectively and eternally responsible for the cruxificion; 'Professor Giff' had claimed that doctors were infecting black youths with the Aids virus; 'Ice Cube' had recommended that the listener should shoot a white Jew, and so on. [*Allgemeine Zeitung*, (Mainz), 15 February 1992.]

10   It was thought in the 1960s that dismantling the sacred would inevitably—and fairly quickly—cut the ground from under the feet of profanity. To take trivial examples: Pornography would soon lose its point when there was complete openness about sex. Swearing would cease once the taboo was lifted from the tabooed words. Peeping-Toms, with their desire to look at other people having sexual intercourse, would disappear once sex was as open and free from taboo as eating.

11   Leo XIII, Encyclical Letter *Rerum Novarum*, 15 May 1891, para. 14, p. 9.

12   *Sunderland Echo*, 14 January 1992. This discussion is not about the 'success' in examination terms of *schools*. It is about the success of *pupils*. Schools with poor examination results may be doing a better job than schools with good results. It can be argued, and may be empirically shown, that such-and-such a school with bad examination results was still doing as good or better a job in equipping its pupils with academic qualifications with which to enter the competition for jobs in the labour market. The 'value-added' to the raw material with which it is presented is the only relevant measure of the *school's* performance. (The substantial inability to effectively demonstrate 'value added' appeared in educational jargon in the early 1990s as 'the yet underdeveloped science of contexualizing examination results' in order to 'correct the crude statistical base'.) But to the extent that the school is exonerated from failure, to that extent the seriousness of the pupils' alienation from the school and other institutions of society is enhanced.

A 'bad academic school' may even, though it is the rare school that has ever demonstrated this, compensate for low academic achievement by high achievements in other equally or more important areas of life.

Arnold, in reforming the 'licensed barbarism' of the public schools of the early nineteenth century, put intellectual ability only third, behind religious and moral principles, and gentlemanly conduct. Stratchey remarks that 'there can be little doubt that Dr. Arnold's point of view was shared by the great mass of English parents'. (Strachey, L., 'Dr. Arnold', *Five Victorians*, London: Reprint Society, 1942, p. 439.) All that Squire Brown wanted for Tom from his school days was that he would turn out to be 'a brave, truth-telling Englishman, and a gentleman, and a Christian'. (An Old Boy [Hughes, T.], *Tom Brown's School Days*, London: Ward, Lock, no date, p. 69.) But no one says that Rugby did not do a good job with the intellectual development of the boys as well.

13   *Sunderland Echo*, 6 January 1992. This was alongside the main front-page report for the day, of the ram-raiding of four premises in the town earlier in the morning, on a wine and spirits store, two clothing stores, and a television and radio shop.

14   *Evening Chronicle*, 24 June 1992.

15   *The Sunday Times*, 19 July 1992.

16   During the seven-month-long miners' strike of 1926 there was, it is true, one incident perpetrated by a few desperate men, whose actions had results far more serious than they had intended, an incident unequivocally condemned in the general mining community. This was the derailment of the Edinburgh-Kings Cross 'Flying Scotsman' at Cramlington, Northumberland. Probably the best-known incident occurred in July 1925, a faint echo of innocence in a harsh age. The Bishop of Durham, Hensley Henson, had made a speech that made him unpopular with the miners. On the day of the Durham Miners' Gala an unfortunate substitute, Bishop Welldon, was spotted walking by some miners. He was attacked with sticks and stones, and the cry went up 'Duck him!' But before the miners could jostle him into the Wear he was protected by some policemen. A police launch was called, which took him to safety from the river bank. (The normal story is a distortion of this—that Hensley Henson was thrown into the river.) Chadwick, O., *Hensley Henson*, Oxford: OUP, 1983, p. 167.

17   Typically, this attitude and terminology stem not out of any local culture, but from 'fans', imitatively out of an international fashion for a particular brand of commercial music. In this case the relevant fashion in 1992 was for 'rap', in which the rapper's women were referred to as 'bitches' and 'whores'. The worst of the rap images of women were presented by such U.S. bands as 'Niggers with Attitude' and '2 Live Crew'. A 1992 rap of the group 'Gheto Boys' celebrated the imagined rape and murder of a woman, who was then posthumously again 'raped'. Two American all-females acts have adopted the insulting names for women of the male rappers, 'Bitches with Problems' and 'Hos [whores] with Attitude'.

18 Amber Films [Newcastle], in association with Channel 4, British Screen and Northern Arts.

19 3 February 1992. Two days later the same programme reported, at the other end of the social scale, that undergraduates at Oxford's all-female Somerville College were generally protesting about the proposal to make it co-educational. One interviewee said this was because male students were 'immature' as well as 'obnoxious'.

20 Benda, J., *La Trahison des clercs* (1927), translated as *The Betrayal of the Intellectuals*, Boston: Beacon, 1955.

21 *Ibid.*, p. 156.

22 Tawney, R.H., *The Acquisitive Society*, London: Bell, 1921.

23 Horkheimer, M., and Adorno, T..W., *Dialectic of Enlightenment*, London: Allan Lane, 1947, p. 3.

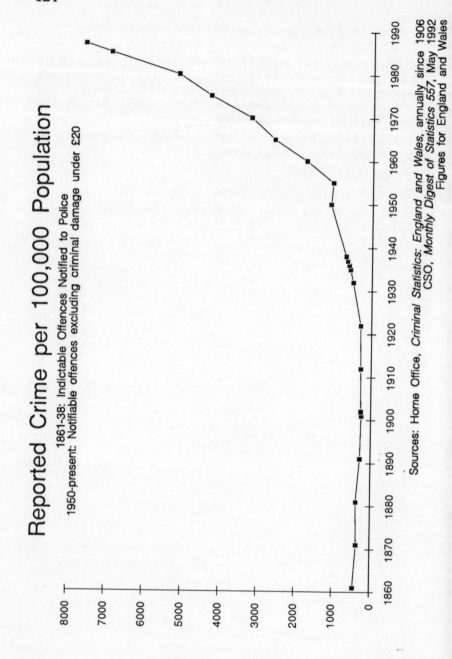

Reported Crime per 100,000 Population

1861-38: Indictable Offences Notified to Police
1950-present: Notifiable offences excluding criminal damage under £20

Sources: Home Office, *Criminal Statistics: England and Wales*, annually since 1906
CSO, *Monthly Digest of Statistics 557*, May 1992
Figures for England and Wales

Appendix

Families without fathers

See *General Household Survey No. 20, 1989*, London: HMSO, 1991. Lone-mother households as a proportion of all households with dependent children more than doubled from 8 per cent in 1971 to 17 per cent in 1989. Though the current figure of over 25 per cent in the U.S.A. had not been reached [Kiernan, K. and Wicks, M., *Family Change and Future Policy*, London: Joseph Rowntree Foundation and FPSC, 1990], in Europe only Denmark had a higher proportion of lone parents than Great Britain [Roll, J., *Lone Parent Families in the European Community*, London: FPSC, 1989]. In what was Western Germany the number of children under the age of 18 with no father present rose from 107,000 in 1975 to 220,000 in 1990. (»Zahl der ledigen Mütter nimmt zu«, *Frankfurter Allgemeiner Zeitung*, 14 May 1992.)

Living together without marriage

By 1989 7 per cent of 16-24-year-olds and 10 per cent of 25-34-year-olds had made their living together and the potential of parenthood into their own private affair, i.e. they were cohabiting. See also, Haskey, J., and Kelly, S., 'Population Estimates of Cohabitation and Legal Marital Status', OPCS, *Population Trends 66*, London: HMSO, Winter 1991.

Conceptions outside marriage

According to OPCS, *Population Studies*, Autumn 1990, in 1988 41 per cent of all conceptions took place outside marriage, as compared with 25 per cent ten years earlier. The rate of births outside marriage had more than doubled in the same decade from 11 per cent to 26 per cent.

Births outside marriage

The percentage of births in England and Wales which were outside marriage remained for decades in the nineteenth and twentieth centuries at around 4 or 5 per cent, with the exception of the period around the time of both World Wars. It peaked at 6 per cent in the 1914-18 war, and at 9 per cent in the 1939-45 war. The ratio fell again after each of these peaks, so that in the early 1950s the percentage of births outside marriage was still only slightly higher than it had been fifty years earlier. It then began to rise slowly until 1979, when it started to rise steeply, so that by 1989 it had reached 27 per cent of all births. CSO, *Social Trends 21*, London: HMSO, 1991, p. 43.

Between 1961 and 1989 the proportion of children born within and outside marriage to mothers under the age of 20 almost precisely switched over from 53:13 to 13:48.

Birth occurrences inside and outside marriage, GB:

Mothers aged under 20

	Inside	Outside
	000	000
1961	53	13
1971	68	24
1981	34	29
1985	23	41
1986	20	44
1987	17	46
1988	16	49
1989	13	48

Birth occurrences inside and outside marriage

All mothers

	Inside	Outside
	000	000
1961	859	53
1971	797	73
1981	614	89
1985	584	139
1986	572	155
1987	574	174
1988	566	194
1989	549	202

Fathers leaving the household

The underlying divorce rate in the 1980s continued to increase. Though now the rate of increase was modest, in 1988 151,000 couples divorced, more than one half of whom had at least one child under the age of 16. In total in 1988 148,000 children under 16 were affected by a divorce in their family. [*General Household Survey No. 20, 1989*, London: HMSO, 1991.]

If divorce rates were to persist unchanged at 1987 levels, 7 per cent of children could expect divorce in their family by the age of 5, 12 per cent by the age of 8 and 24 per cent by the age of 16. Some feeling of the magnitude of the cultural change in two generations can be derived from the remarks of the eminent sociologist of his day, R. M. MacIver. Referring to the total English divorce figures of 4,018 for the year 1928, he pointed out that the national newspapers treated this monstrously high figure as a national scandal! *Society: A Textbook of Sociology*, New York: Rinehart, 1937, p. 216.

Other Health and Welfare Unit Publications

1992 and the Regulation of the Pharmaceutical Industry

April 1990, £6.95. ISBN 0-255 36259-5

MIKE L. BURSTALL

Dr Burstall's study of the regulation of the pharmaceutical industry by the EC considers the pros and cons of national as opposed to European regulation. Among the issues he examines are price and profit regulation, patent law and product licensing on grounds of both safety and efficacy, each of which holds lessons for other industries which trade in Europe.

The Emerging British Underclass

May 1990, £5.95. ISBN 0-255 36263-3

CHARLES MURRAY, FRANK FIELD, JOAN C. BROWN,
ALAN WALKER & NICHOLAS DEAKIN

'Britain has a small but growing underclass of poor people cut off from the values of the rest of society and prone to violent, anti-social behaviour, according to a report published today by the Institute of Economic Affairs.' *The Times*

'Mr Murray ... cites three early-warning signs from the US — rising illegitimacy, violent crime, and refusal to work — which are increasing in Britain.' *The Daily Telegraph*

Equalizing People

July 1990, £3.95. ISBN 0-255 36262-5

DAVID G. GREEN

'The IEA ... is gearing up for another crusade.' *Financial Times*

Morality, Capitalism and Democracy

September 1990, £3.95. ISBN 0-255 36266-8

MICHAEL NOVAK

'A leading American intellectual ... with the message that capitalism is not simply a successful ideology; it can also capture the moral highground. Professor Novak's aim is to produce a set of ideals by which democratic capitalist societies may judge themselves.' *The Independent*

———————◆———————